Walking
Deeside, Donside and Angus

Clan Walk Guides

Walking

Deeside, Donside

and Angus

Walking Scotland Series
Volume 13

Mary Welsh
and
Christine Isherwood

First published by Clan Books 2004
Reprinted 2008

ISBN 978 1 873597 20 0

Text and Illustrations
© Mary Welsh
and
Christine Isherwood
2004

Clan Books
Clandon House
The Cross, Doune
Perthshire
FK16 6BE

Printed and bound in Great Britain by
St Edmundsbury Press Ltd, Bury St Edmunds, Suffolk

Authors' Note

Roebuck

Please remember on all these walks:

Wear suitable clothes and take adequate waterproofs.

Walk in strong footwear; walking boots are advisable.

Carry the relevant map and know how to use it.

Take extra food and drink as emergency rations.

Carry a whistle; remember six long blasts repeated at one minute intervals is the distress signal.

Do not walk alone, and tell someone where you are going.

If mist descends, return.

Keep all dogs under strict control. Observe all 'No Dogs' notices—they are there for very good reasons.

Readers are advised that while the authors have taken every effort to ensure the accuracy of this guidebook, changes can occur after publication. You should check locally on transport, accommodation, etc. The publisher would welcome notes of any changes. Neither the publisher nor the authors can accept responsibility for errors, omissions or any loss or injury.

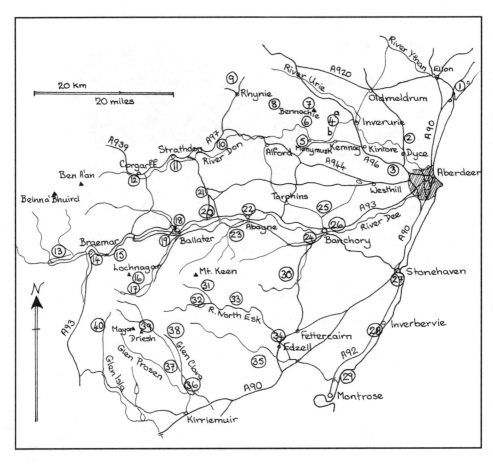

Area of the walks

Contents

1

Sands of Forvie

Park in the free car park at the Stevenson Forvie visitor centre, grid ref 033289, Little Collieston. Forvie lies 16 miles north of Aberdeen and is reached by B9003, which turns east off the A975. Buses stop by request at Collieston road end, and then it's a 20 minute walk to the visitor centre.

Huge spreads of sand were dumped by glaciers in the area, at the end of the last ice age, some 15,000 years ago. Through time sea levels fell and exposed the sand. Later coastal winds blew it inland much as it is seen today on this walk. The earliest dunes formed in the south of Forvie 2000 years ago. Gradually the sand moved north to reach Collieston by about 1700. As you walk among the southern dunes it's easy to imagine that you are in the Sahara—sometimes a very cold desert!

Hackley Bay

Near the remnants of the salmon fishing station at Rockend are the remains of a medieval settlement. The walk takes you past the roofless ruin of **Forvie's 12th century kirk**. By the 15th century the whole settlement had disappeared under sand. According to local legend, the village was overwhelmed when three sisters placed a curse on it after they had been cast adrift in a leaky boat to deny them taking up their inheritance. However the sisters did reach dry land. Then the curse whipped up a terrible storm that continued for nine days and nights. By the time it had abated the sand had buried the village.

Walk 1

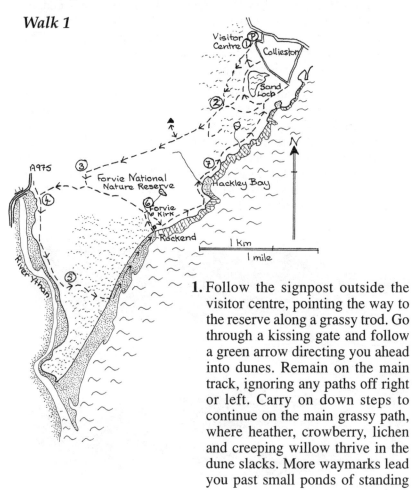

1. Follow the signpost outside the visitor centre, pointing the way to the reserve along a grassy trod. Go through a kissing gate and follow a green arrow directing you ahead into dunes. Remain on the main track, ignoring any paths off right or left. Carry on down steps to continue on the main grassy path, where heather, crowberry, lichen and creeping willow thrive in the dune slacks. More waymarks lead you past small ponds of standing

water and on through marram grass and contorted bushes of willow, the haunt of meadow pipits, stonechats and skylarks. After nearly a mile from the centre and some distance beyond a large pond you reach another waymark.

2. Pause here to locate your ongoing route. This is where you leave the main track and bear right on a distinct track, marked by landrover wheels. You soon reach a Y-junction, where you take the left branch to carry on steadily uphill onto a sandy, rocky ridge from where you have a superb view of a huge bay, with Aberdeen a smudge on the far side. To the right you can see a trig point on the skyline. Then descend a little and watch out for a narrow path right. This leads through heather and then grass, along the little ridge, to come to the trig point, 180 ft/57m, on its delightful grassy top, where you might wish to take your first break and enjoy the extensive view. Then return along the ridge to rejoin the landrover track, where you turn right to begin crossing the moor of Forvie. The way continues ahead through mainly heather and then descends through more sand dunes. It then goes on through a vast area of heather and, after a mile from the trig point, the track leads to an area of humpy dunes.

3. At the edge of the heather and before the humpy dunes, turn left along a grassy track, soon to join a much wider track, where you turn right. Follow the descending way over more sand dunes, with a fine view of the estuary of the River Ythan and the small town of Newburgh on the far bank. The grassy trod leads down to a gate, where you leave the nature reserve. Walk ahead from the gate along a wide track to a junction of tracks by the estuary, where you turn left.

4. Continue ahead beside the lovely river, following a blue waymark. Here look for swans, black headed gulls, redshanks, large groups of eiders, curlews, goldeneye, cormorants, oyster catchers, mergansers and many terns fishing. Go through the next kissing gate back into the nature reserve. Enjoy the closely cropped path just above the Ythan. Remain on the banking and look ahead for an enormous hill of golden-red sand, quite free of vegetation, and an extraordinary sight. Follow the path as it leads slightly inland to pass along a narrow valley between towering dunes to come to the foot of a row of steps. At the top of these you can see more of the vast expanse of sand. Then a waymark directs you left through

more dunes to a notice board. This requests that from April to September you remain on the path, outside the taped way, so that the breeding colony of four different types of terns can get on with their nesting undisturbed.

5. Follow the marker posts and cross walkways helping you to progress over the soft sand. And then you can see a fenced area inside the protected area. The fencing is electrified, powered by solar panels, to deter foxes from destroying the eider eggs and chicks, also tern eggs especially those of the little terns. After climbing a steepish sandy slope a waymark directs you ahead and then on to the seashore and an incredible stretch of golden sand. Turn left and follow the occasional blue arrows, directing you for ¾ mile along the sands in the direction of Rockend. As you near the rocks, cross the Old Kirk Burn and then climb the deep, sandy track, left, between dunes. Continue on the waymarked track through the scant remains of the old salmon fishing station and go on up the slope until you reach the next waymark on the right. This directs you right for the driest approach to the new footbridge over the burn. Climb the steps beyond, and go on up to come to the ruin of Forvie's 12th century kirk, where you will want to idle for a while.

6. Then carry on along the waymarked path to come to a wide track that runs along the cliffs, where you turn left. Eventually it winds round, high above Hackley Bay. If you wish to descend the almost sheer cliff face make sure you use the very long, steep flight of easy steps down onto the sheltered sands from the south. You need to leave the bay by the same way as this is the only safe route out.

Otherwise follow the well made fenced, stepped path and then the walkway as it winds high above the bay. Climb a long flight of steps, which takes you up to higher cliffs, with more dunes on top. On the ledges of sea cliffs kittiwakes and shags nest.

7. Then the wide track moves inland a little through more dunes. Stroll on along the red waymarked trail to descend steps to a footbridge and up the other side. The path continues inland, with the small fishing village of Collieston in the distance, to come to a gate out of the nature reserve, which you ignore. Bear left to continue with the fence to the right, following the green and red waymarked posts. Head on towards Sand Loch, which you can just glimpse. Continue on a walkway. On the large blue pool you might see whooper swans. Press on along the path as it winds round the loch. Ignore the next kissing gate out of the reserve and continue on a short distance to come to the kissing gate, taken earlier, to return to the visitor centre.

Eiders

Practicals

Type of walk: Choose a good day for this long, exciting, stimulating walk.

Distance:	7 ½ miles/12km
Time:	4–5 hours
Maps:	OS Explorer 421, OS Landranger 38

2

The Formartine and
Buchan Way: Dyce to Ellon

Park at Dyce Station, grid ref 885128. To reach this follow signs directing you along Station Road from the centre of the town. The car park is signposted as the start of the long distance recreational path. Dyce lies north-west of Aberdeen.

Largely using the **trackbed of a disused railway** this route, a permissive right of way, runs from Dyce to Maud via Udny, Ellon, Auchnagatt, and from Maud to Peterhead via Mintlaw and to Fraserburgh via Strichen. Its current length is 39 miles/66km (Dyce to Peterhead) or 41 miles/66km (Dyce to Fraserburgh). It is open for cyclists, walkers and horse-riders. To complete this linear walk,

Viaduct over R. Ythan at Ellon

from Dyce to Ellon, 14 miles long, you will need to use two cars or ask a good friend to pick you up at Ellon. Or you could complete short sections and return the same way.

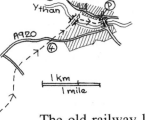

Walk 2

The old railway line took the names of the two provinces, Formartine and Buchan, through which it passed.

1. Leave the parking area by the north end to join a signposted tarmac path, which takes you through a suburban park. The way is soon lined by tall bushes of broom. In early autumn watch out for swallows that use the track as a flight path for chasing flies only rising from near the ground as they come near to you. Go on to cross a red metal bridge and beyond you have your first glimpse of the River Don, which you cross by a wide stone bridge. Gradually the track takes you out into rolling countryside but not yet completely away from the noise of planes and helicopters from the airport at Dyce. As you walk, look left to see Mither Tap on the skyline, your companion for much of the walk. Eventually the noise of air transport is left behind and you can hear the curlews calling from the pastures about the line. Carry on along the track, where hazel, rowan, and willow line the route. Go on to pass the Goval Burn, hidden deep in vegetation. Watch out for grey partridges hurrying across the track. Cross a road, once bridged by the railway, to pass under a pleasing stone bridge, with the village of Newmachar coming into view.

13

2. Press on the quiet way as it runs along a high embankment, which winds in a long graceful curve. Enjoy the fine views before the way moves into a high-sided cutting which, through much of the year, is a floral highway. Go on past some new housing, the retaining wall on the left and that on the right, once part of Newmachar station. The pleasing way then makes another curve as it passes through another deep cutting. Here, at the right time of the year, look for goldfinches feeding on thistle heads. The track then carries on through quiet pastures of barley and red-legged partridges fly from one field to another, over the line. Along the fine curve look out for elephant hawk moth caterpillars, laboriously crossing the track. They feed on the ubiquitous rose-bay willow-herb where among the plants they will pupate. Pass through the remnants of Udny Station and go on under a bridge. Cross the Tarty Burn on an old stone bridge among trees and then descend, fairly steeply, to cross a road to go through a parking area.

3. After passing the Mains of Orchardton carry on through Logierieve Wood. Among the trees is a signposted parking area for people wishing to join the track here. To do so cross the road and walk right. Just before the road bridge, descend easy-to-miss steps to the path, now deep within high banks, lined with bushes. The path is now grassy and easy to walk and has seats along the way.

Grey Partridge

4. Take care as you approach the A920—there was once a railway bridge here. Today the traffic comes fast from the left and, from the right, it comes fast too but from round a sharp bend and is not seen until the last minute. Then stroll on along an embankment above the housing estates on the edge of Ellon. Look ahead to see the ruins of Ellon Castle beyond the town. Cross the viaduct over the Ythan river and, just beyond, take the waymarked right turn to descend steps to the riverside. Walk on along the good path with the flower-lined river to your right. Leave the riverside just before a red metal footbridge, where you turn left, and then cross, right, a footbridge over a ditch. Bear right alongside a rugby pitch or across a long stretch of grass, both routes keeping parallel with the Ythan. Eventually they both join and you go on along a right branch beside the river. Pass under a road bridge and then under a picturesque stone bridge soon to reach the car park, with toilets and where, hopefully, your second car is parked.

*Red Admiral and
Small tortoiseshell*

Practicals

Type of walk: A long level walk through flat and rolling farmland. The surface is excellent but quite hard! A change of shoes or boots, half way, helps.

Distance:	14 miles/22.3km
Time:	5–6 hours
Maps:	OS Explorer 421, OS Landranger 38

3

Elrick Hill and Brimmond Hill

Park in Tyrebagger Sculpture Trail car park, grid ref 848111. To reach this leave Aberdeen by the A96 and follow the signs for Inverness. After leaving the built-up area, past the airport roundabout, turn left at the top of the hill on to the B979 and follow signs to Tyrebagger.

These **two delightful hills** lie on the outskirts of Aberdeen but except for rare glimpses of the city it rarely impinges on this walk. At one time most of the land around Aberdeen would have been covered in dense woodland. Clearance of the forest land started over 3000 years ago to provide timber for building, fuel for cooking and to open up ground for grazing cattle and growing crops. Following widespread tree felling, much of the land became covered by heather moorland. In the late 18th century most of the moorland was brought into cultivation by farmers. Today the vegetation of both hills is slowly changing. With little grazing the heather is being invaded by gorse, broom and bracken. Birch and rowan trees are also beginning to spread in.

Forest Sculpture, Tyrebagger

1. Leave the back of the car park by climbing a fairly rough path through trees. Follow the red, brown and yellow ringed waymarkers. A short distance along, before you turn right to follow the yellow and brown waymark, read the ingenious plaque which explains the artist's ideas behind his work. Then walk down the path to the sculpture, which consists of seats, a table and a footbridge over a pool. Beyond, follow the signpost for Elrick Hill. Wind left (the right turn leads to several picnic tables) to walk a railed way through woodland and then up through mixed heather, bracken and sparsely scattered rowans.

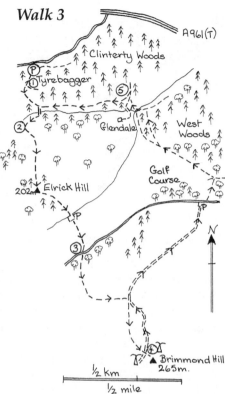

Walk 3

2. Bear left following the yellow and brown waymarks, with a wall to your right. When the yellow waymark route goes off left, follow the brown marker up through heather to the top of Elrick Hill, 666 ft/202m. It has a lovely flat summit, with picnic tables, and a great view all the way from the sea to Lochnagar. Then continue on to descend the path through heather and bracken, into woodland, in the direction of Brimmond Hill, with its three tele-communication masts. Look for the grassy glade, to your right, with more picnic tables, within a ring of gnarled and twisted Douglas fir. After a pause in this delightful spot follow the brown arrow to descend a long flight of steps into a small car park and go ahead to a narrow road.

3. Cross and climb up more steps to follow a narrow, overgrown path to a stile. Beyond, bear slightly right to ascend through rampant gorse. Ignore all right or left turns and carry on up rough pasture on a faint path. This brings you to a stile over a fence. Once over, walk

right as directed by a waymark to join a tarmacked road. After a few steps, right, take the brown waymarked path, on the right, which leads on uphill towards the heather surrounded summit, 873 ft/266m. At a Y-junction, bear left to climb to the highest telecommunication station. Cross the rough service road and walk through the heather to the trig point, a mound of stone and more picnic tables. Enjoy the incredible view of the Hill of Fare, Clachnaben, Bennachie and to the North Sea beyond Aberdeen.

Great Spotted Woodpecker

4. Return to the service track, just crossed, and start your descent. Soon it becomes reinforced and goes on down to a kissing gate into a small car park. Cross the road, beyond, and bear right for a few steps and take the signposted way, on the left, into West Wood and signposted, Tyrebagger 1 ¼ miles. Cross a metalled track, which gives access to the golf course and go on. Stroll on and on with open ground through the trees to the left and, woodland or clear-fell, to the right. Just before the path drops down a slope, and half way along below some magnificent beeches, turn right to walk a narrow grassy path. Follow it as it descends to a wider track, signed 'Path', and turn left. Walk on to a signpost, and turn right. Cross a foot-bridge and climb up a wide track, bearing slightly right and upward, through more majestic beeches. At the waymark, cross a track, left, and climb a little to another signpost, where you walk left.

5. Stride the track through woodland, passing several sculptures which you might wish to visit, and then continue on to the car park.

Practicals

Type of walk: Clear well signed footpaths lead to the summits of two modest hills, from where the views are most pleasing.

Distance: 4 miles/6.5km
Time: 2–3 hours
Maps: OS Explorer 406, OS Landranger 38

Easter Aquhorthies

Park in the car park for the recumbent circle, grid ref 733212. To reach this leave the A96 at Inverurie's Blackhall roundabout, by a minor road, going west, signed Burnhervie. Just over half a mile along this road, and where it swings left, go ahead up a narrow lane to use the second car park on your left.

Easter Aquhorthies is derived from the Gaelic meaning 'Field of Prayer'. The Easter Aquhorthies stone circle, believed to have been constructed by farmers, living in the Garioch region, possibly dates back to the 3rd millennium BC. The stones on the north-east side of the circle are the smallest and they increase in size round the circle until the two tallest are on the south-west side and flank the recumbent. This is wedged and chocked to make it

The Recumbent Easter Aquhorthies Stone Circle

level. It has been suggested that the circle was used for astronomical measurements, using the recumbent stone as an artificial horizon for observing the rising and setting of certain stars or the moon and that this helped farmers with the timing of their agricultural activities. It is also possible that the circle was used as a centre of worship; it may also have been a burial ground. The circle is situated on a hill, a mile north of the River Don, and from it there is a good view of the surrounding countryside.

Walk 4a

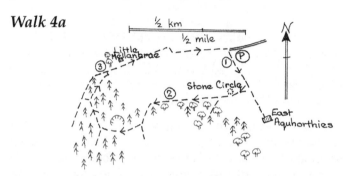

1. Leave the car park by a gate in the top right corner and walk left along a hedged reinforced track which soon becomes metalled. A short distance along take the signposted right turn to follow a little path leading to the gate into the site of the circle, where you will want to linger. Then return through the gate and turn right along the excellent continuing path. The way soon begins to descend, pleasingly, between rampant vegetation in summer, with tall trees

Sedge warbler

to the left. Where the way divides take the right branch, with a turf wall on either side. Ahead is a spectacular view of Mither Tap.

2. Carry on, ignoring paths to the left, then curve left on the main path through mature forest. At a Y-junction take a right turn and press on along the good track. Go on past a quarry, ignore a left turn and walk on to wind right of a barrier across the track. Turn right to walk a narrow path edged with wych elm and beech. The path goes on between gorse and spruce to the right, and fine beeches to the left, beyond which are open fields. At an old turning space at the end of a forest rack turn left to walk a narrower path, through bushes, to step over a low wire and out onto a track.

Reed bunting

3. Turn right and walk the airy way. Continue up the lane to pass a cottage named Little Mellanbrae. As you near the car park the track becomes lined with great reed where you might hear sedge warblers trilling and see reed buntings. The car park is just beyond and is shaded by several lofty beeches.

Practicals

Type of walk: Not to be missed. It is short and quite delightful.

Distance: 1 ½ miles/2.5km
Time: 1 hour
Maps: OS Explorer 421, OS Landranger 38

NB *You may wish to do walk 4b on the same day as this walk as they are only a couple of miles apart.*

4b

Burnhervie to Fetternear

The parking area, grid 734191, lies a quarter of a mile south of Burnhervie, close to the suspension bridge (Shakkin' Briggie) over the River Don and reached by minor roads north from Kemnay.

Fetternear House was burnt down in 1919. Started in the 16th century, Fetternear, the seat of the Leslie family, has been described as 'an unusually interesting example of the transformation of a Laird's Tower into a Nobleman's Palace and thence to a Gentleman's Seat'. But little remains today and the ruin should not be approached but looked at from the 'weak bridge'. The house was built on the site of a medieval Bishops's Palace.

Fetternear House

1. From the parking area walk back along the 'no through road'. Go past a cottage on the right and then, just before a house on the left, turn left along its gravelled drive. Walk beside the house to pass through a gate beyond it, with a notice asking you to close it. Stroll the continuing track across fine parkland to go through another gate. Carry on along the splendid track through open beech and birch woodland, with the River Don to your left. Ignore any left or

right turns and remain on the delightful way. Then the track moves into dense woodland, where at the right time of year, the flowers of the lime trees perfume the air.

2. Go through the next gate and carry on beneath fine beeches and then an avenue of lime. Carry on the gated way to reach a small grassy triangle. The track on either side of this brings you to a wider track, where you turn left and cross a bridge. At the T-junction walk right beneath limes and elms and then turn right to cross another bridge, signed 'weak bridge', to the access track of the stunning ruin of Fetternear House.

3. Return by the same route. Remember to turn right at the triangle of tracks.

Walk 4b

Lime

Practicals

Type of walk: A there-and-back walk on a good track through very pleasing deciduous woodland.

Distance: 4 ½ miles/7.2km
Time: 2 ½ hours
Maps: OS Explorer 421, OS Landranger 38

NB *You may wish to do walk 4a on the same day as this walk as they are only a couple of miles apart.*

5

Monymusk

Park in the car park at Monymusk behind the village hall, grid ref 685154. The village lies west of Kemnay and is reached by a turn, north, off the B993.

The pretty village of **Monymusk** is situated where the River Don emerges from the gorge between Bennachie and the Menaway range. Sir Archibald Grant was responsible for the planned 18th century village square. He rebuilt the houses, built most of the roads and introduced cottage industries to create employment and for education. He also reformed the church singing by forming a choir which could sing the hymns and psalms right through. The Grant Arms Hotel in the square was formerly an 18th century coaching inn. The two largest houses immediately in front of the church were built for the land steward and the headmaster of the school. There might have been a wood and plaster church where

Monymusk

today's St Mary's stands—its tower dominating the glorious square. It is believed that the present chancel may date from around 1160. It is the oldest church still in regular use in the north-east. It is certainly one of the most fascinating.

Walk 5

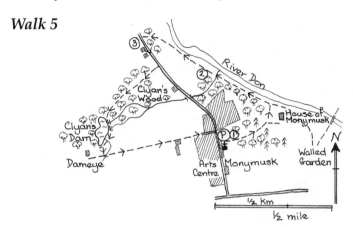

1. Leave the car park behind the village hall and walk towards the lovely church then turn left. Go down past the cemetery, then through a gateway, and follow the continuing metalled way, with a great variety of trees on either side, set behind high deer fences. Carry on until you reach the side of the sweetly flowing River Don. Enjoy the grand view of Mither Tap, the most dramatic top of Bennachie. If you wish to visit the garden centre and enjoy a cuppa, turn right. Otherwise turn left to pass through tall red gates to enter the conservation area. Carry on beside the dancing river where you might spot a heron fishing. The excellent track passes through delightful woodland, the haunt of a lively stoat and many rabbits.

2. The track gradually moves away from the river and the way opens out, with a pasture to the left. It soon returns you into woodland with many ornamental trees. Sir Archibald Grant—see above—is reputed to have planted 48 million trees in his lifetime. Through the trees, to the right, you can see the Don hurrying from the hills, to the north, and then curving gracefully to flow beside the track you have just walked. Press on to gates to the road. If you can't puzzle out how to pass through, try sliding the small gate on the right, to the left.

3. Cross the road and walk left for a short distance, past several cottages, to arrive at a small car park on the right, which you pass through. Go on along a grassy track through Clyan's Wood. Look for the four magnificent redwood trees and then carry on until you spot a wooden bridge, on the left, which you cross. Stroll on a wide track beneath trees to come beside a delectable pond, called Clyan's Dam, where ducks idle. Pass a well placed seat and then take the good short track, left, to join a farm track, where you turn left. Dawdle on along the track and continue where it becomes metalled. Join the main road through the village to return to the parking area. Perhaps you will have time to visit the interesting Arts and Craft centre situated in an old church at the far end of the small village.

Stoat

Practicals

Type of walk: This is a short but glorious walk that should not be missed. It starts from a picturesque village, with a fascinating church, passes through splendid woodland and comes close to the River Don and a large pond.

Distance: 3 miles/5km
Time: 1 ½–2 hours
Maps: OS Explorer 421, OS Landranger 38

Bennachie—Millstone Hill

Park at Donview car park, grid ref 673191, where there are toilets. To reach this, go through Monymusk by taking a right turn (north) off the B993 from Kemnay and Inverurie. At the crossroads turn right again to go over the River Don. Then take the next two left turns and continue for two miles along the north bank of the Don to reach the parking area.

From the car park you may be able to see a dead tree towering up above all other trees. On its top is a huge nest of twigs. If you have binoculars you might see the nest occupants: young **ospreys** and/or the adults. The nest has been used for several years. If lucky you may see an osprey fishing. It hovers over the water and then plunges in feet first to catch its fish. When it emerges it shakes itself as it flies away.

Osprey

Mither Tap from Millstone Hill

1. Go through the trees at the back of the car park to a tall post supporting several coloured waymarks. Follow the olive-green arrow to climb through Norway spruce to come to a forest road. Cross and go on steadily ascending the good path opposite. Then the way levels and passes through a clear-fell area, where tiny rowans and birch thrive. Cross a forest track and go on the waymarked yellow route through extensive clear-fell. Millstone Hill lies to your left at this point and the path swings round towards it. Carry on beside conifers to cross another forest road.

2. Go on along a red arrowed route through larch, where you might spot bullfinches. Follow the gently rising path to a seat in a tiny glade in the forest. Then go on up to emerge from the trees, following a path that bears right, above the forest, along the heather and bilberry clad slopes of Millstone Hill. As the path begins to climb you have a wonderful view of rural Donside and, ahead, you can see Mither Tap. Press on the lovely, easily climbing path and follow it as it winds, left, and levels a bit before climbing a granite-pitched way. Go on along a short boardwalk from where you can see the cairn on top of the hill's granite summit. Follow the gentle ascent, noting a path that leads off right, to the top where you will want to pause to enjoy the spectacular view. If the weather has changed go on over the top and descend a clear path that takes you down to the car park.

3. This walk takes a longer route for the return. Descend from the summit by the upward route to take the path ignored earlier and now on your left. Carry on down a good path, with long stretches of boardwalk taking you over wet areas, where bog asphodel thrives between the heather. Follow the path as it enters the forest and then descends a pleasing ride between conifers. Follow this path as it winds left (ignore a track going off right) to stroll a level way following brown waymarks. Join the yellow waymarked forest road, ignore a right turn and go on for a very short distance to turn left down a forest track, waymarked yellow.

4. At its end bear sharp left on a forest road, still following yellow waymarks, with delectable glimpses of the River Don below. At the brow of the road, bear left and watch out for the waymarked right turn. This path, with blue and yellow waymarks, descends gently round the edge of old clear fell. Follow the path as it winds round left beside a heavily lichened wall. Close by scattered mature deciduous trees have escaped the axe and many oaks have been planted. The blue and yellow trail then crosses the open area, left, and descends through the forest. Here the escape route, off the summit, joins this descending track. Wind round a traffic barrier and just beyond follow the blue and yellow arrows along a narrow path, left, through conifers. This leads into the forest once more and through the trees behind the car park.

Practicals

Type of walk: An easy well waymarked route, through forest and heather slopes with wonderful views of the surrounding countryside and the Bennachie range. The summit is magic.

Distance: 5 miles/8km
Time: 3 hours
Maps: OS Explorer 421, OS Landranger 38

7

Bennachie—Mither Tap

Park at Back of Bennachie car park, grid ref 661245. To reach this leave the A96, 9km north-west of Inverurie, to take the B9002. Go through the village of Oyne and 1km further on take a track, on the left, into the parking area.

Bennachie is a long granite ridge standing up from the fertile lowlands of the Garioch, smoothed by ice action during the last glaciation. Some parts of the granite were harder than the main mass and resisted the ice; these form the higher tops of the ridge, some of which have rocky outcrops called tors. The exposed granite on the tors weathers into a characteristic 'woolsack' pattern, like slabs piled on top of one another.

The **iron-age fort**, which surrounds the summit of Mither Tap, possibly dates from sometime between 500 BC and AD 500. It must have taken an enormous amount of labour to build the fort. Thousands of tons of granite boulders would have to have been carried up the hill to build the 20 ft thick outer and inner walls of the rampart, which stretch from cliff to cliff

Mither Tap

and surround the whole top of the hill. There are remains of round houses inside the wall, and a well, but most local people probably lived in round houses or hut circles on lower ground and used the site on Mither Tap as a refuge, possibly from the invading Romans.

Walk 7

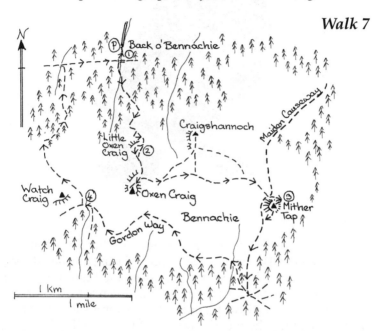

1. Leave the car park, at the far end, by a pleasant path which winds up through the forest beside a small burn. At the forest road, turn right, cross the burn and then turn immediately, left, to continue up the other bank of the stream on a good path. Ignore any left or right turns and follow the path as it recrosses the burn and winds on uphill. Emerge from the trees and go on across heather moorland on a gravel path edged with blocks of granite. The way then zigzags gently uphill until it reaches a signposted right turn which leads to the tor, Little Oxen Craig. There is an old quarry on the side of the tor from where granite was quarried for lintels. Then scramble up, easily, onto the granite slabs of the top. Pause here to enjoy your first fine view to the north.

2. Walk south across the slabs to join a small path which winds through heather, soon to join a wider one, heading for the next tor, Oxen Craig. The way is well made and has steps up the steepest section.

31

Buzzard

Oxen Craig has a trig point and a stone shelter; at 528m it is the highest point on Bennachie. Here you will want to enjoy the superb view. Then return by the same path from the trig point, along the narrow top of the tor, but head off right before reaching your upward path taken earlier. Descend quite steeply for a short distance and then go on along the broad ridge towards Mither Tap, which rears up, spectacularly, at the far end. At the time of writing the path appears to be in the process of being upgraded. Here you may wish to make a detour to Craigshannoch, another tor, by taking a path that leads left to and from it. Carry on to the foot of Mither Tap. Ignore paths going off left and right and continue straight on. The granite blocks of the huge tor look like walls but they are entirely natural. Press on along the path that climbs and circles round to the far side, where it turns up towards the tor again. Follow the path as it passes through an enormously thick wall—this one man made. Here look, right, in the thickness of the wall to see a chamber, and the remains of dwellings on the flatter inside area. These are traces of the ancient hill fort. From here climb an indistinct path, which slants up a great heap of stones and then follow one of the many paths up onto the summit, where there is a trig point. Here enjoy the fine views south to Mount Keen and Braid Cairn, and Lochnagar.

3. To continue the walk, descend, south, down sloping rocky slabs, then curve round right to pass through another gap in the ancient wall and go on down to join a major path. Turn left and follow it downhill. It soon leaves the heather moorland and enters scattered trees, which become denser as the slope eases. At the bottom of the hill you are back in the forest and have reached a junction of five paths. Take the one immediately to your right, which is signposted GW for Gordon Way. Press on along this path, through forest, climbing gradually to the upper limit of the trees where it traverses the hillside above them and there are crags above to the right. Then the signposted way (GW) zigzags quite steeply upwards, eases and turns sharply left to continue as a delightful terrace path below the top of the ridge, with views out over Donside and Deeside.

4. Look out for the path marked with a blue arrow, on the right, and take this to climb up to the top of the ridge. The tor to your left is Watch Crag and to your right is Oxen Craig. Go straight on between them and down the other side to the top edge of the forest. On entering the trees, turn right, almost immediately and walk along just inside the trees until you reach a spur of the hillside. Here the path turns left and goes downhill to cross a clear-felled and replanted area. At the bottom the path meets a forest track, where you turn right and follow it to the small burn crossed on your outward route. Turn left on the path beyond the burn and return to the car park.

Practicals

Type of walk: Delightful. The route is all on paths or tracks, which are generally in good condition. The walk varies from forest to open heather moor and takes in a superb hill fort. The views are stunning.

Distance:	8 miles/13km
Time:	4–5 hours
Maps:	OS Explorer 421, OS Landranger 38

8

Knock Saul via the Gordon Way

Park at Suie car park, grid ref 548232. To reach this leave Alford by the A944, going north, and once across the River Don take the country lane, continuing north, in the direction of Clatt. The parking area lies on the right at the top of the long hill.

The **Gordon Way** is a long distance footpath. When completed, this will be a 20 mile/32km walk across the Bennachie range, from Rhynie in the west to Essons car park in the east. At present it is open from Suie to Essons, a distance of 17 miles/27km.

The harsh screech of the **jay** and a flash of white calls the walker's attention as the bird dodges out of sight. On the ground it hops jauntily. When disturbed it flies quickly and speedily into cover. It is partial to acorns, beech mast and nuts. In summer it is an egg-thief but it also destroys pests such as wire-worms and grubs of the destructive winter moth. Jays have a white crest streaked with black, the rest of the head, breast and back are a soft fawn. The chin, throat, belly and the area surrounding the base of the tail are white, contrasting sharply with the brown-black tail. It has beautiful black, white and blue barred feathers on the wing.

Boundary stone

Walk 8

1. Take the left turn immediately inside the car park, from where you can see Tap o'Noth, with a faint outline of the fort on its summit. Then walk on along the pleasing path, lined with heather as it passes through conifers which lie back on either side from the way. Go on past, on the left, Suie Cairn and an old boundary stone and carry on. As you progress on to the high heather moorland of Suie Hill 1320 ft/415m, enjoy the glorious view of Clachnaben, Braid Cairn and Mount Keen. Look back to see Beinn A'an in the Cairngorms. Take the little path, on the right, which leads through the heather to another boundary stone, this one with J carved on one side and W on the other. Return to the main path and press on to pass through a gap in the transverse fence across the heather.

2. As you move into more trees the path runs beside a low wall almost lost to sight below vegetation, where bilberry and cowberry thrive among the heather. The conifers then close in beside you—take care as you step over the many roots nearly hidden by the needles from the trees. Carry on along the path as it narrows and heads out into an oblong-shaped clearing, set around the edges by conifers. Jays abound here and, in the autumn, chickweed wintergreen colours the verges. Soon after the conifers close in again, a waymark directs you left and onto a forest road. Here turn right. In 45m take an easy-to-miss waymark directing you left through a wide expanse of heather with, at the time of writing, young spruce still allowing views of patchwork fields to the north. Then descend the path through birch and follow it as it makes comfortable, wide, grassy zigzags down to wooden steps to join a forest road through the Den of Drumgown.

3. Turn left to walk a few steps to a Y-junction. Take the right branch and turn, in a few more steps, right, along a narrow path, edging

Jay

more conifers. The way begins to ascend in more wide zigzags into the dense plantation. At the waymark above the zigzags you are directed left and then left again along a wide rutted track. Then the way winds slightly left and then right to emerge from the trees— to help you find your way through this short dark section of the walk some trees have been felled and you should follow the tree stumps. There are several waymarked posts, but more would help! The final waymark directs you across a lighter area to another forest road. Cross and climb straight up a rough, and sometimes slippery fire-break in more conifers. At the top of this steepish climb, and just beyond the edge of the trees, is a welcoming waymark. Climb uphill through extensive heather to another waymark. Beyond, a short walk leads to the trig point on Knock Saul 1334 ft/412m. Here too is an old cairn in which has been built a rough shelter. The summit area is heather-clad, remote, lonely and quite delightful. It has a similar boundary stone to those seen earlier and, surprisingly, a picnic table. Pause here and enjoy the superb views.

4. Return through the heather and then down the ride to the forest road. Cross and go through the dark conifers, following the waymarks and tree stumps. Zigzag through the trees to join the lower forest road through the Den of Drumgown. Turn left and left again to take the wooden steps, on the right, at the start of the zigzags, which ease your way uphill. Cross the heather and spruce area at the top to come to the forest road. Turn left here and stride on to a Y-junction where you take the right branch, contouring along the edge of the forest, with a superb view ahead of Mount

Keen. Go on into the forest and follow the road until it ends at a turning area, just over half a mile from where you joined the road. Press on ahead along a narrower, rough path, for under a quarter of a mile. This could be wet after heavy rain as it climbs steadily through conifers. Pass between posts of a fence, a continuation of the fence passed on Suie Hill, and go on a couple of steps to a T-junction.

5. Turn left and descend for a quarter-of a mile, down a wide ride, until you can see open land through a few remaining trees. Turn right and walk a wide ride that climbs steadily but gently through heather and more conifers. After nearly a mile the path brings you out to the car park.

Chickweed Wintergreen

Practicals

Type of walk: A pleasing forest walk that takes you up onto a heathery summit. As you go you should see goldcrests, siskins, coal tits, robins and crossbills in the conifers.

Distance: 5 miles/8km
Time: 3 hours
Maps: OS Explorer 420, OS Landranger 37

9

Tap o'Noth

Use the car park at the foot of the hill, grid ref 480284. This is reached by taking the A941 north-west from Rhynie for 2 ¾ miles. The parking sign directs you, right, up a narrow lane to the parking area on the left.

At the top of the hill, 1851 ft/563m, stands the remains of a splendid **hill fort**, the size and shape of a football pitch and the second highest fort in Scotland. This large grassy area is enclosed by a circular wall of stone. Part of this shows vitrification, many of the stones being fused together by great heat. It is not known whether they were fused together accidentally as a result of fire or whether they were packed with wood and burnt on purpose—a process used to strengthen the walls. One possible origin of the name Tap o'Noth is the Gaelic 'taip a'nochd', which could be translated, appropriately, as a look-out top.

A **legend** about the hill tells of a giant, known as Jock o'Noth, who stole the lady love of the neighbouring giant, Jock of

Tap o'Noth

Bennachie. The latter was so enraged by this 'theft' that he hurled a huge boulder and dispatched his rival on Tap o'Noth. The boulder can be seen on the lower slopes.

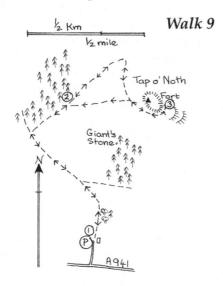

Walk 9

1. Walk up the continuing track from the car park to climb a stile. Carry on up the rough pasture to go through a small wood of beech and pine, keeping parallel with the wall on the left to climb another stile in the top left corner. Beyond follow a path, going left, with dense gorse to the right and a fence to the left, both the haunt of stonechats that sit atop the gorse branches and fence posts. Go with the path as it rises through an open area. Just before a gate into a young plantation, turn right to ascend a wide grassy track. As you climb the moorland, a conifer plantation lies to your left and a vast area of heather stretches up the west side of the hill. Go on to pass a narrow path on the right that climbs quite steeply uphill; you may wish to use this for your route of descent.

Stonechat

2. Press on up the main track, which becomes a little rougher, and then follow it as it winds right and continues as a lovely terraced way. It is along this terrace that the steepish footpath comes in on your right. Follow the track as it winds left and becomes pleasingly grassy. Pause here to enjoy the spectacular views over the surrounding countryside. And then head up the track to go through the wall into the large open space of the fort. Wander around the 'ramparts' and look for the vitrified rocks. Stand by the trig point set in more fused rocks. Note the several circular hollows in the open area, today filled with stone, but believed to be where huts once stood. The views from the summit are superb.

Bell Heather

3. To descend, leave the summit by your upward route and decide when you reach the path, dropping left, whether to take this short cut. It rejoins the main track lower down. Then retrace your outward route.

Cross-leaved Heath

Practicals

Type of walk: All the family will enjoy this pleasing walk.

Distance:	3 miles/5km
Time:	2 hours
Maps:	OS Explorer 420, OS Landranger 37

40

10

Milltown of Kildrummy

Park in the large shady lay-by, grid ref 470178, with picnic tables, beside the A97 at Kildrummy.

Donside is not as well known as Deeside but is equally lovely. Upper Donside could be described as the region's secret valley and it is through this gem that this walk passes. The Don rises in the Grampians at Wells of Don, west of Corgarff, on the slopes of Cairn Culchavie, part of the ridge of Brown Cow Hill. It reaches the North Sea on the north side of Aberdeen.

Kildrummy Castle, reached from the A97, lies a mile south-west from the start of this walk. The thirteenth century ruins stand in a hollow of the hills on the edge of the Don valley. It was a stronghold of the Earls of Mar and the headquarters for organising the 1715 uprising. It is open daily, from 09.30 to 18.30 from April to September. For more information tel 01975 571331.

River Don near Kildrummy

1. Leave by the north end of the lay-by. Cross the A-road with care, and take the narrow road that leads uphill. Bear right to pass a larch tree, on the right, growing on the remains of an ancient burial cairn. Continue to pretty Kildrummy parish church, built in 1805. Wind left before it to climb steps into the kirkyard of St Bride's Chapel, where there are some ancient gravestones. Then after enjoying this peaceful corner, return to cross the A97 and pass through the lay-by, where you have parked. Cross the A-road for the third time and go on along the quiet road in the direction of Milltown of Kildrummy. At Nether Kildrummy, turn left on to a track, which continues beside the River Don.

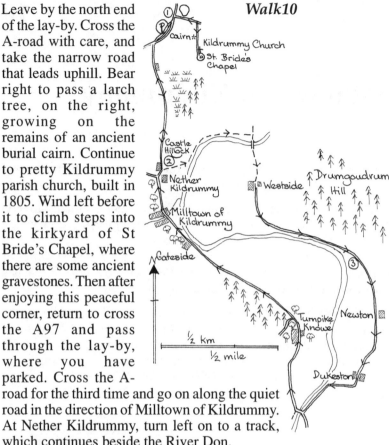

2. Go on along the riverbank where common terns dive for fish. Cross three cattle grids and follow the track to go over a bridge where, in summer, the banks of the Don are lined with bright yellow monkeymusk. Climb the slope beyond, to pass between the house and outbuildings of Westside. Follow the track which soon becomes metalled and passes along the side of the surging river, with conifer-clad Drumgoudrum Hill—the haunt of buzzards—to your left.

3. Eventually you reach the point where the river moves across the valley bottom to flow close below Turnpike Knowe. Between the road and the river is a wide area of marsh, which in high summer is gloriously colourful with monkeymusk, meadowsweet, great willowherb and tufted hair-grass. Go on past Newton farm and by

Dukestone farm. Follow the road as it winds right to come beside the Don once more. Join a slightly wider road, turn right and cross a metal road bridge over the river. Climb uphill to pass Turnpike Knowe farm and then begin your descent towards Milltown. As you go enjoy the delightful hamlet tucked into a graceful curve of the Don. Continue with the river to your right. Ignore the left turn which leads to the A-road and go on past Nether Kildrummy. Retrace your outward route along the quiet road to the A97. Cross and bear right to the parking lay-by.

Monkeymusk and Meadowsweet

Practicals

Type of walk: This route takes you on tracks and quiet narrow roads, virtually traffic-free, which run on either side of the River Don. It is a delightful walk in summer when the fields and river banks are full of wild flowers—in winter this is an excellent low-level walk.

Distance: 5 ½ miles/9km
Time: 3 hours
Maps: OS Explorer 405, OS Landranger 37

11

Bunzeach Forest, Bellabeg with motte and church

Park in the car park, grid ref 354129, at Bellabeg in Strathdon, where there are picnic tables and public toilets. This is reached from Ballater by the A93, A939 and the A944. Or by the A944 up Donside.

Bellabeg lies in the parish of Strathdon, the most mountainous and westerly parish of Upper Donside, with 18 peaks over 2000 ft. To the north are the Ladder hills, to the south Morven and to the west are the Cairngorms. The U-shaped flat-bottomed valley is due to glaciation but the river is relatively narrow and shallow. At one time the River Avon would have drained this way from the Cairngorms but the ice diverted its course north so now it flows into the Spey. Cultivation of the strath is limited to a single tier of farming along both sides of the Don, with forest on steeper slopes beyond. Strathdon church stands on an eminence, dominating five glens.

Strathdon Church

Long ago the churchyard was used as a venue for feuding clans. The name Strathdon means the level valley of the Don.

The **Doune of Invernochty**, lies at the point where the Water of Nochty and the River Don meet. The dun is oval in shape and moulded from a residual mass of fluvial gravel. The summit of the great mound is 250 ft/76m in length, 118 ft/36m wide and 63 ft/ 19m high, surrounded by a deep ditch. At times of stress an ingenious system of canalisation brought water in to flood the ditch. Eight hundred years ago this was the most important fort in Upper Donside until Kildrummy Castle was built. During excavation a stout curtain wall, 2 ft/0.6m thick was unearthed, with an entrance to the south. Within the wall was found the remains of a Norman chapel which served Invernochty until the 17th century.

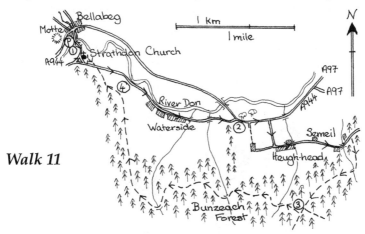

Walk 11

1. Walk out of the back of the car park and continue along beside the River Don. Turn right and cross the bridge over the hurrying water. Follow the road as it winds left and then climbs, right, uphill. Go into the burial ground of the fine Strathdon church and look at the interesting tombstones and the two huge mausoleums. Leave by the back gate, turn right and walk on to join a narrow road, where you turn left. Carry on through the strath on the quiet road, passing scattered cottages and houses, for just over a mile. Enjoy the many small birds to be seen as you go.

2. Join the fairly quiet A944 at milestone 43 and walk right, with fine beeches to the left and pastures to the right. After less than half a mile, take the right turn for Heugh-head. Follow the narrow road

where it swings left and passes the few houses that make up the settlement. Beyond, in early summer, the verge is colourful with a myriad of water avens. Continue for three-quarters of a mile to turn right into the forestry car park at Old Semeil. Go on gently up the continuing rough track. Ignore the track on the left and carry on for about a mile from the car park.

3. At the right turn follow the green arrows along a better track, where you descend a little and then contour on. From here there are good views over and through the trees. Carry on the main track, mostly contouring and then descend gradually. As you go watch out for jays flitting across the way. Go on down through more open larch to a place where the track suddenly becomes grassy and mossy (this is not a cross-roads but looks as if it is going to be). Go on down along the edge of the forest, with fields and the river below.

4. The way continuues above the road walked earlier. Finally it comes down to the narrow road. Turn left to walk to the church, where you bear right beyond it. Walk downhill to retrace your steps to the car park.

Goldcrest

Practicals

Type of walk: A pleasing walk for a windy day, when shelter can be found in the valley and through the forest. Half the walk is along quiet roads and half through forestry.

Distance: 6 ½ miles/10.5km
Time: 3 hours
Maps: OS Explorer 405, OS Landranger 37

12

Corgarff and old castle and military road

There is a large car park at Corgarff Castle, grid ref 254089. Alternative parking, which would reduce the road walking, is up the first part of the Old Military Road (a track) in a large clearing on the right, with hard standing, grid ref 263084. To reach both places take the A939, which runs from Ballater to Tomintoul, over the Lecht road. Corgarff Castle is on the left, going west, before you reach the Lecht, and the entry to the parking area is through a gateway (no gates) with heraldic animals on it, beside a house. The castle is signposted.

The **Old Military Road** ran from Fort George on the Moray Firth to Braemar via Corgarff. General Wade planned the route but it was built under Major William Caulfeild in the mid 18th century following Wade's departure from Scotland. A second military road was built from Corgarff to Aberdeen, part of which also has public right of way status.

Corgarff Castle

In 1507 James IV granted the forest of Corgarff to Alexander, First Lord of Elphinstone. **Corgarff Castle** was built soon after, standing at the head of the Don Valley some 445m above sea level and commanding the road links to the Dee, the Avon and the Don. The castle was later passed to the Forbes family of Towie. In 1571 at Tillyangus the Forbes met a party of Gordons from Auchindoun Castle and a fierce and bloody encounter followed. The Gordons, supporters of Mary Queen of Scots, went on to take Corgarff Castle for Mary and, when Margaret Forbes refused to surrender the castle was set alight burning all 24 inhabitants. In 1645 the Marquis of Montrose, campaigning for Charles I, occupied the castle before the Battle of Alford. It was later owned by the Earl of Mar, leader of the 1715 Jacobite Rebellion. The Jacobites had burned the castle in 1689 to deny it to the government and government burned it again in 1716 as a reprisal against Mar. The star-shaped curtain wall was built in 1748 when the castle was taken over by the Hanoverian government and garrisoned. It was to be used as a centre for tracking down Jacobite rebels. Its final use as a garrison was between 1827 and 1831 when a captain, subaltern and 56 men were stationed there during the campaign against whisky smuggling. It was given into state care in 1961 and restored by Sir Edmund Stockdale.

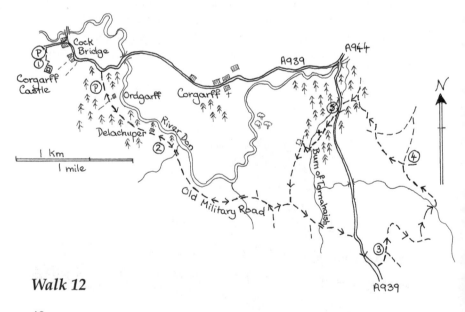

Walk 12

48

1. Turn right out of the car park and go up to see the castle. It is worth looking at even if all you can do is walk round the outside—it is open only from April to September. It closes for lunch. Then return down past the car park and turn right on the main road and walk with care. Take the second track on the right, about ½ mile/¾ km farther on, signposted 'Old Military Road' and is also signed for Jenny's Bothy. The track goes through fairly dense conifers, with an attractive mossy wall on the right.

Mountain hare

Continue past the alternative parking place and cross a track. Go on past Delachuper and Jenny's Bothy, both standing in a pleasant grassy clearing on the left. On the right is open heather moor.

2. Follow the track as it curves round the hillside above the Don. Until recently this was a delightful green grassy track but unfortunately it has now been insensitively bulldozed. As this track is an ancient monument there is a lot of bad feeling locally about it. Continue on to cross three old packhorse bridges, which have been restored by historic Scotland and are well worth looking at. Climb up from the last bridge to reach the A939 and turn right to walk for 300m, using the verge as much as possible. Cross to the east side of the road and take a landrover track leading uphill.

3. Go straight ahead where the main track goes round a hairpin bend to the right. Continue on this more vegetated track contouring round a spur of the hillside. On the far side begin to climb more steeply. Beyond a row of grouse butts look ahead across the valley of the Allt na Gaothain and note where the line of a track slanting along the hillside comes down to the burn at the right-hand end. This is the point you are making for. Look carefully on the left of the track you are on for any sign of a path going down the hillside— the one shown on the map has really ceased to exist on the ground and you will have to pick your own way. Fortunately the heather is short and, lower down, is intermingled with grassy patches and

49

there are animal tracks. In places you can see the old path as a bank and a ditch, especially down near the burn. Cross the burn, which is very small here, and go up the more obvious path on the far side which slants steadily up the hillside on a shelf. After a few metres you come out of the rushes and deep heather into shorter vegetation and walking becomes much easier. Watch out as you go for mountain hares. The views open out and are splendid. You can see over the whole wide basin of the upper Don, with Beinn A'an, and its unmistakable granite tors, on the skyline, to the south-west.

4. At a cross of tracks, where there is a new grouse butt, turn left to descend an old grassy track along the top, and then down the right-hand side, of a spur. The scar of another newly bulldozed track disfigures the hillside below and to your right. Descend to this track and cross it. Then take a pleasant grassy old track down into a small valley, where you might spot roe deer feeding down by the burn. Carry on down the path into scattered trees and then across an open area at the top of a plantation. Go through a thin belt of trees and then down the right-hand side of another clearing. Join the forestry track at the bottom and turn left to walk out to the road.

5. Turn left and walk up the road for 200m to a small road on the right, signed to the Catholic Church of Our Lady of the Snows. Cross and go up this road. The church is tiny and has a cottage attached to the side of it. Walk left round the garden fence and

Roebuck

50

follow the track beyond, which is green and mossy and winds along beside the Burn of Tornahaish. At the Y-junction take the right branch. This brings you to a ford which you will have to cross. Wind up the track through the forest to a T-junction by a ruined building at the top. Turn left and press on along a path that comes out of the pines and contours along the heathery hillside. It then runs along the top of the broad spur to join the Old Military Road. Turn right and retrace your steps to where you have parked.

Red grouse

Practicals

Type of walk: This is a long walk, much of it along estate tracks but some is pathless. There are a few short sections on roads. After heavy rain you will have to wade the ford—not deep but you will get wet feet.

Distance: 10 miles/16km
Time: 5 hours
Maps: OS Explorer 405, OS Landranger 37

NB *This is a grouse-shooting area. Avoid between August 12 and October 20 and keep dogs on leads at all times. The military road, however, is a right of way and can be walked at any time of the year.*

13

Glen Quoich and Glen Lui

Park just before the bridge over the River Quoich in an old quarry, grid ref 116910. Or cross the bridge and park on the verge beside the road end at Allanaquoich, grid ref 118912. To reach both leave the A93 in Braemar, signed Inverey. Continue past the Linn of Dee and along behind Mar Lodge to the road end.

The magnificent cock **capercaillie** is a large heavily built bird with a curved whitish bill. It has a grey-black 'dress' and legs feathered to the toes. Across its breast is a metallic green patch and above the eye is a long vermillion wattle. In spring it displays extravagantly for the benefit of the admiring hens it has attracted. Capercaillies feed on young leaves, buds, shoots, pine needles, fruits, berries, caterpillars and insects. They make short, swift strong

Linn of Quoich

flights, often low, and then drop down quickly. Many die by flying into deer fencing and this is why the National Trust has placed orange or green strips on fencing to prevent them, and also black grouse, from flying into it and killing themselves.

The present Mar Lodge was built in 1898 from sketches by the then Princess Royal who married the Earl of Fife. The previous building was at Corriemulzie across the Dee and was burnt down in 1895. Just recently the Mar estate was sold to the National Trust for Scotland. They are doing good things on the estate, such as removing the bulldozed track up Beinn a'Bhuird and constructing deer fencing to allow regeneration of the pinewoods. They are also very encouraging to walkers.

Walk 13

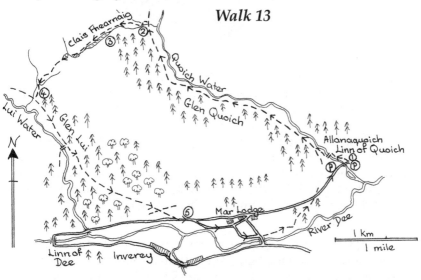

1. From the first parking area suggested, continue along the road over the bridge and turn left off the track to follow a clear path up beside the River Quoich. Notice remains of buildings and an old mill race. Go on along the bank of the river into open pine forest and then pause to enjoy the lovely waterway which here flows in a deep-cut gorge and, a little higher up, comes down in a superb water spout where it has worn a narrow cleft through the rock. Cross the bridge over the river and follow a minor path for a short way along the far bank to see more waterfalls and waterworn holes in the rocks. This is the Linn of Quoich. Return from this dramatic place to rejoin

53

Red deer

the main path from the bridge. Climb up the bank to the top of the river terrace and continue along the edge above the river, which lies well below. A short distance along join a track coming in from the left. Go on along the pleasant sandy way, where the glen opens out and the track winds up among open pine and birch, interspersed with heather. Look for red and black grouse and also for siskins and crossbills in the pines; red squirrels are common and the cones from which they have stripped the scales litter the ground. Carry on up the glen where the immense bulk of Beinn a'Bhuird comes into view ahead.

2. Two miles from Linn of Quoich, the track comes down to cross a small burn. Beyond the burn, turn left up a somewhat rough path towards a hut in a fenced enclosure. Swing left on the path and follow it as it winds round and climbs gently uphill outside, and to the left of, the fence. Follow the path over the heather moor towards a rocky gully, Clais Fhearnaig, ahead. Pause here and look at Beinn a'Bhuird, with Beinn A'an, another giant, just peeping over its shoulder.

3. Carry on the path as it leads into the gully, with a small shallow lochan on your left and cliffs above on your right, where you might spot peregrines. Go on up the cleft, changing to the left side where it bears slightly right, with another pool on your right. Carry on past the pool and follow the path as it climbs again and comes out on the right side of, and well above, a wider boggy valley. Continue on the path as it crosses a burn and then descends gently into Glen Lui. Away to the right is a large area of pine woodland surrounding Derry Lodge and behind it rise slopes, with more scattered trees, that lead up to the distant Derry Cairngorm.

Peregrine

4. Turn left on the track through Glen Lui where you might, at the right time of the year, see lots of red deer on the river flats. Go on to a sturdy bridge over the river. Do NOT cross the bridge but take the less well used track which goes straight ahead and then winds up the hill for a short way through open birch and pine once more. Eventually you reach a stile over a deer fence which you climb into denser forest. Then the forest opens out again. Ignore any tracks off to the left or right and go on into the Dee valley and descend gently to the road behind Mar Lodge.

5. Turn left on the road, then take the first right, down to Mar Lodge, where there is a sign welcoming walkers. Follow the paved road round to the front of the lodge and turn right to walk away from it towards the river. At a T-junction, just before Victoria Bridge, go ahead to take a track opposite. Follow this through woodland, passing through several gates, to rejoin the minor road beyond Cragan Cottage. Turn right and walk downhill to where you have parked.

Practicals

Type of walk: This a glorious walk, all on paths or tracks, and with only a very little climbing.

Distance: 9 ½ miles/15.4km
Time: 5 hours
Maps: OS Explorer 404, OS Landranger 43

14

Creag Choinnich

Park in the car park, grid ref 152913, at Braemar. To reach this turn off the A93 in the village onto a minor road, signed Village Centre and Inverey. Fifty metres further on turn left before Strachan's General Store and Wine Merchant.

Creag Choinnich (1764 ft/538m) is the small hill behind Braemar. The area is owned by the Invercauld Estate who welcomes walkers and at the time of writing is in the process of putting up interpretive signs by the paths. The walk starts from Braemar, the eastern gateway to the Cairngorm mountains. It is also where the famous Braemar Gathering is held on the first Saturday in September each year. The walk comes close to the entrance of Braemar Castle. For opening times telephone 013397 41216.

Path near Lion's Face

The walk takes you takes you close beside the fine cliff of the **Lion's Face**. Unfortunately you can't see the resemblance from the walk. You need to be on the other side of the valley from where it really does looks like a lion's face—when the light is right. In autumn, when the larches above it turn gold, it looks as if the lion has a glorious mane.

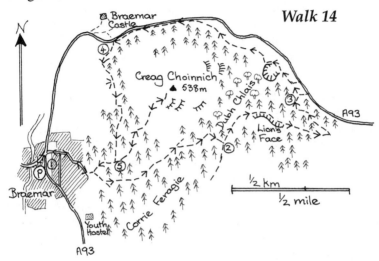

Walk 14

1. Leave the car park by steps at the far side to come to the A93. Cross and take the small road, Hillside Drive, almost opposite, beside St Margaret's Church, signed 'Creag Choinnich'. At the top of the road it comes close, on the left, to woodland. Go through either the gate, or the stile, in the corner of the fence, into mature pine, with moss and bilberry below. Look for coal tits and siskins in the trees, and there is a good chance of seeing a red squirrel. Almost immediately the path forks and you need to take the right branch, signed to Lion's Face and Cromlins Circuit. Follow the path as it begins to climb into younger, denser pine trees. Ignore an indistinct path off to the right and go on climbing gently. Then follow the path as it contours round the hillside, with open scrubby pine to the left. At a vague Y-junction take the right branch. Go through a gap in a low wall and turn right to walk along beside it until the path joins a well made grassy track. Turn right to look at the ruins of a house beside the track. This is where a gamekeeper and his wife lived and were visited by Queen Victoria, who brought them gifts of tea and tobacco.

2. Go back to where you joined the grassy track and go on straight ahead along a path signed Lion's Face. On your left the ground falls away and soon you are walking along a delightful wide terrace path above a steep gorge, with birch and larch around you. At a bend in the path the view opens up and you can see across the Dee to the enormous mansion of Invercauld House, the home of the Farquharsons of Invercauld who have been major landowners in this area for centuries. Pause here on the seat to enjoy the superb view. Follow the path on round the corner below the Lion's Face cliff and continue on into dense pine woodland, crossing and recrossing two burns.

3. At the bottom of the slope there is a large gate giving access to A93. Just before you reach this, turn off left to take a signed and waymarked path towards a local authority depot. Then turn left, when the path joins the road, into the depot and walk through it, taking care if there is any traffic. Beyond the huts and piles of stone there is a substantial quarry. Carry on towards a tall waymark and go left of the mound on which it stands. Go on round the corner to pass another waymark and climb a small path leading out of the depot and up round the side of the quarry. Follow this as it turns away into the wood and contours round above the road, finally coming down to pass through beech trees just behind the wall of the road. Braemar Castle comes into view on the far side of the road. Go through the kissing gate in a fence. If you would like to visit the castle take the gate out onto the road and another opposite.

Capercaillie

4. Otherwise turn left and climb the hill, which is stepped where it is steep. Admire the fine views of Upper Deeside, through scattered mature birch trees. At the top of the hill is an interpretive board telling you about the geology, history and wildlife of the area. Walk on, with the forest to your left, to a gate across the narrow track. Do not go through but climb the stile on your left, which takes you back into the forest. Continue parallel with the fence until it turns away and then follow the waymarkers through the trees. Follow them downhill but take care if there has been any forestry work as the path can become less than clear. Make sure you can see the next waymark at each decision point.

5. At a T-junction you may wish to turn right to return to Braemar. This walk turns left to climb Creag Choinnich. The path is obvious and well made, with more steps in steeper places. Above the trees the hillside is open and covered with heather and bearberry, with scattered pines and birches and great boulders of granite. At the top is a huge cairn and a stunning view, from the Cairngorms to the north round to the Glen Shee mountains in the south. The River Dee curves round the foot of the hill below. Return by the path of your ascent, continuing down to the gate and stile where you entered the wood. Then go back down the road to the car park.

Bilberry

Practicals

Type of walk: A very pleasing walk through glorious woodland, with many fine views.

Distance: 4 ½ miles/ 7.4km or 3 ½ miles/5.8km if you miss out Creag Choinnich.
Time: 2–3 hours or 2 hours
Maps: OS Explorer 404, OS Landranger 43

15

Ballochbuie

Park in the new car park up the short side road to Keiloch, off the A93, just east of the Invercauld Bridge, grid ref 188913. At the time of writing it costs £2 a day to park. The money goes for path maintenance. There is a toilet.

The native pinewoods of Scotland are now reduced to a scattered remnant, but in parts of Deeside it is possible to see what they may have been like. Huge old pioneer trees, with widely spreading branches, are known as 'Granny Pines', and they provide much of the seed for the young trees. Where groups of trees have all grown together they are much straighter with shorter side branches. A natural pinewood has trees of all ages, growing in scattered groups of differing densities. It should also have many seedling pines, but where deer numbers are high the seedlings have all been eaten and

Bridge, Garbh Allt Waterfalls

there is no regeneration. Attempts are now being made to keep deer numbers down or to exclude the deer from parts of the forests in order to allow the pines to regenerate. Some have now appeared above the heather which have substantial trunks and are therefore old, but have previously been grazed off at heather level. Ballochbuie pinewood was bought by Queen Victoria in 1879 to prevent it being felled. It is now managed as a conservation area.

Walk 15

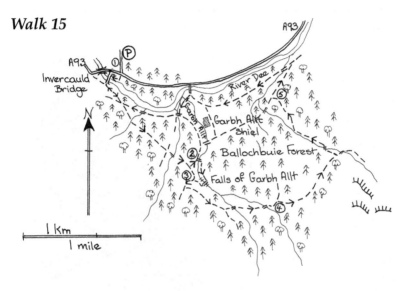

1. Return from the parking area to the A-road and cross. Take the path that goes down into the woods and soon brings you out onto the bank of the River Dee. Turn right and walk up to the old Invercauld Bridge, built under the auspices of Major William Caulfeild who succeeded General Wade, as part of a military road linking Fort George on the Moray Firth with Coupar Angus via Braemar and Glenshee. Cross the bridge and turn left at the T-junction just beyond, to follow a pleasant sandy track which runs uphill into the pinewoods of Ballochbuie Forest, with the river to the left. At the next junction go straight ahead, slightly uphill, and then on through the trees. Cross a track just before the Glenbeg Burn and then the bridge over the hurrying water. Carry on ahead. There is a fenced enclosure on the right, to exclude deer so that the trees can regenerate. The fencing has thin slats, close together, to make it visible to black grouse and capercaillies.

61

2. At a fork in the track ignore the gated right branch and go a short distance downhill on the left branch. Then take a footpath on the right down towards a wooden bridge over the Garbh Allt. Go through a gate and cross the Garbh Allt, pausing as you go to admire the tumbling burn with its waterslides and deep pools. On the far side of the bridge, turn right and follow a narrow path through heather and bilberry above the burn. Soon the path turns a corner and, in front of you, descend the magnificent Falls of Garbh Allt. Cross the elegant cast iron bridge spanning the burn above the main fall and follow the path to rejoin the track.

3. Turn left and walk on to the next track junction to turn left again. Continue upward into more open pine forest. Admire the many huge pioneer trees and keep an eye open for red squirrels, black grouse and capercaillies. As you continue to climb you can see through the open woodland to the hills beyond. Look for the big corries on the side of Lochnagar and the pointed peak of The Stuic. After a quarter of a mile take a track going off left towards the Garbh Allt once more, which you cross on a bridge, rather more rickety than the previous

Blackcock

ones. Cross the next tributary on another bridge and follow the path as it climbs into open heather moorland, with some scattered pines.

4. Where the path forks, take the right branch to climb to a gate in the deer fence, and go on through scattered woodland. Carry on along the path as it contours the side of the hill, Cnapan Nathraichean. Pause to enjoy the views over Deeside and out to the Cairngorms. Press on where the path descends gently to come to a fork beside a small burn, where you take the left branch and go downhill, with the burn on your right. Cross the stream on a small wooden bridge and stroll on down the other bank. Stride on the path as it turns away from the stream and follows the deer fence downhill to join a forest track.

5. Turn right along the track and in another quarter of a mile turn very sharply left on a path through pines open at first, then becoming very dense. Soon there is a large open unfenced field on your left, where deer graze. At the far side are the cottages of Garbh Allt Shiel. Beyond this field, turn right on the track which has come past the cottages. Carry on until you reach a white painted cast iron suspension bridge over the Dee. Do NOT cross the bridge, but turn sharp left. Cross the Garbh Allt on a wide bridge just above its confluence with the Dee and follow the track to come to a bridge over the Glenbeg Burn. Turn right to return to Invercauld Bridge.

Scots pine

Practicals

Type of walk: Easy walking on tracks and clear paths through a splendid old pine forest, with many fine views, waterfalls and footbridges.

Distance: 6 miles/9.8km
Time: 3 hours.
Maps: OS Explorer 404, OS Landranger 43 and 44

16

Lochnagar

Park at the end of the minor road up Glen Muick, grid ref 310852. This is reached from the B976 which runs along the south side of the River Dee, just south of Ballater. Then turn off onto the minor road east of Bridge of Muick. The car park is well laid out and at the time of writing it costs £2 to park all day. The proceeds go towards path restoration and maintenance.

Lochnagar (3,789 ft/1,155m) a Munro, is the highest point on the Mounth Plateau, the range of hills and high moors separating Deeside from the lowlands of Angus. It lies entirely within the royal estate of Balmoral. It is a splendid mountain, with its north side gouged into fine corries above the ancient pinewoods of Ballochbuie. From Deeside there are excellent views of this fine hill.

Lochnagar

It was this mountain that inspired **Prince Charles** to write a children's book called 'The Old Man of Lochnagar'. It was a favourite walk of Queen Victoria. Lord Byron said of the mountain

England! Thy beauties are tame and domestic
To one who has roamed o'er the mountains afar.
Oh for the crags that are wild and majestic!
The steep frowning glories of dark Lochnagar.

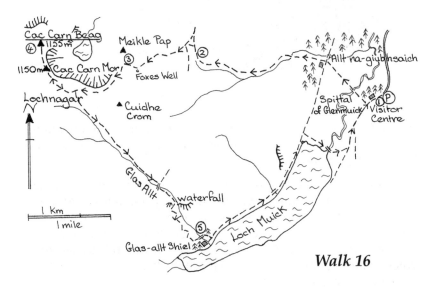

Walk 16

1. Turn left out of the car park and walk down past the visitor centre, which has displays about the wildlife of the area. Just beyond, turn right along the signposted Lochnagar Path. Walk down the sandy track that crosses the wide flats below Loch Muick, where you might spot deer. Listen as you go for the calls of lapwings, curlews and common gulls. Where the track swerves right, go straight ahead on a footpath and then, a few yards further on, cross another track at a T-junction. Follow the signpost directing you up through a delightful open pinewood until it reaches a burn, where the path turns left and goes along the river bank. The way then emerges from the wood onto heather moorland. Ford the burn on stones and climb steadily up the good path on the other bank, with the burn now deep in a gully to your the left.

2. After nearly a mile the path levels out and comes to the watershed, where the gully suddenly becomes shallower. Leave the main path and go on along a clear path that diverges left. Follow it where it runs downhill for a short distance and then curves round at the beginning of the long ascent to the col between the main hill and

Ptarmigan

Meikle Pap. Here you might see ptarmigan, grouse and mountain hares. On reaching the col, walk over to the far side to look into the magnificent corrie.

3. Turn left and ascend steeply beside the edge of the corrie. At the top of the climb continue over the bouldery, tundra-like ground round the edge of the corrie to Cac Carn Mor, which has an impressive cairn. From here descend a short distance and then climb up to the summit, Cac Carn Beag. It is a delightful granite tor, which requires a mild scramble to reach the top, with its trig point and view indicator.

4. Return from the summit by retracing your steps to Cac Carn Mor. Half a kilometre beyond the cairn branch right, onto a path, which makes a long descending traverse into the valley of the Glas Allt to join a good path. Here, at the right time of the year, you should

Snow Buntings

see more ptarmigan and many snow buntings. Follow the path down, with the burn to your right, until you can cross a sturdy wooden footbridge. Turn left and go on down the other bank of the burn, which tumbles in a series of spectacular waterfalls. Carry on the path as it makes wide zigzags down the hillside, to come to a pinewood.

5. Cross the bridge and go on down through woodland to reach the main track along the north shore of Loch Muick, which here is dramatic with high enclosing hills on both sides. Turn left along the track and follow it to the boathouse at the foot of the loch, where you turn right onto a lochside path. At the far side of the loch climb up to another track and turn left. Follow it back to the car park.

Mountain azalea

Practicals

Type of walk: This is a superb climb, not too difficult nor is it exposed. The stretch up from the col, called the Ladder, with Meikle Pap away to the right, is the steepest.

Distance:	12 miles/19km
Time:	6 hours
Maps:	OS Explorer 388, OS Landranger 44, Harveys Lochnagar

NB All the usual provisos about climbing Munros apply. Access is fine all the year round but in the stalking season, August to October 20, you should return by your route of ascent.

17

Loch Muick and Dubh Loch

Park at the end of the minor road up Glen Muick, grid ref 310852. This is reached from the B976 which runs along the south side of the River Dee, just south of Ballater. Then turn off onto the minor road east of Bridge of Muick. The car park is well laid out and at the time of writing it costs £2 to park all day. The proceeds go towards path restoration and maintenance.

The whooper swan's bill is mainly lemon-yellow, with a wedge of this colour extending into the black tip beyond the nostril. Whoopers seldom arrive in this country before October and if undisturbed linger until June. On the water the bird carries its neck stiffly erect. When feeding it upends, submerging its head and fore parts to obtain aquatic weeds and molluscs. When the bird flies it flogs the water for a short distance and then once under way flies with great speed, its neck extended and its wings making a whistling sound. This is the reason for it often being called the whistling swan. It also makes a musical honking noise and is quite vocal, unlike the mute swan.

Loch Muick

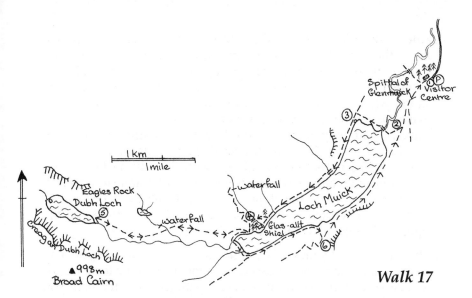

Walk 17

1. Leave the car park and go down the road past the visitor centre, set beside a pine wood. Then continue along the track and go round a vehicle barrier. Walk straight ahead on a track raised slightly above the valley bottom. Ignore the path going off right along the side of the wood. Soon the lovely loch comes into view in its deep glacial trench of hills. Lochnagar is hidden behind its lower outliers on the right. Look for red deer here, especially early in the morning or evening.

2. Turn right at the next path junction to walk across the end of the loch, crossing the outflow on a long wooden bridge. Continue on the pleasant sandy path, watching out for dippers on the stones. Go past a boathouse by the end of the path and climb the bank beyond to turn left on to a good sandy landrover track.

3. Follow this for 1 ½ miles/2 ½ km, passing through scattered birch and heather and crossing burns by substantial wooden bridges until you reach another pine wood. This surrounds Glas-allt Shiel, a house once used as a lodge by Balmoral Estate and now a holiday cottage. Go through a gap in the wall round the wood and immediately turn right off the track, onto a pleasing path which winds uphill through the pine trees. Near the top of the wood cross a wooden bridge over the Glas Allt and continue ahead, ignoring the path which goes up beside the burn (the path used for your descent on the Lochnagar walk).

69

4. After a short level stretch the path begins to descend again, just inside the wall—be careful crossing the many tree roots, especially if the ground is wet. Go through a gap in the wall on the right and on down over old sleepers to join another path down by the loch shore, where you turn right. A few metres on you may wish to make a two mile, each way, diversion to Dubh Loch. If so take the stalkers' path on your right and follow it as it climbs up the north side of the valley. Ford the Stulan Burn and admire its splendid waterfall. Then continue climbing, with the Allt an Dubh-loch gleaming and foaming as it slides over slabs of granite to your left. Press on and, where the slope eases, the Dubh Loch lies spread before you enclosed between the crags of Eagle's Rock, on the right, and Creag an Dubh-loch on the left.

5. The path now becomes less distinct and wet. From here you may wish to continue to the sandy beach at the head of the loch, or just retrace your steps down the stalkers' path to rejoin the path you left earlier, where you turn right. Carry on just above the water of Loch Muick and cross two burns on bridges. In autumn and winter there may be whooper swans on the loch. At the far side of the valley the path climbs gently, to the left, up the hillside and then contours. Ignore the path coming in on your right and walk on above the loch until the good path begins to climb again and curves round into the valley of the Black Burn.

6. Join a rough bulldozed track and turn left to cross the burn, which seethes and foams below the bridge. Continue on this track, which soon becomes sandy and easy to walk, for 2 ¼ miles/3.5km to the visitor centre and then back to your car.

Practicals

Type of walk: A fine route round a lovely loch, with a dramatic optional climb to another loch set in even more wild scenery.

Distance:	Around Loch Muick 7 ½ miles/12km. Around Loch Muick and the diversion to the sandy beach of Dubh Loch 11 ½ miles/17.5km
Time:	3–4 hours or 5–6 hours
Maps:	OS Explorer 388, OS Landranger 44, Harveys Lochnagar

18

Craigendarroch

Park in the Station Square at Ballater, grid ref 370958, or in the large car park behind the church.

Craigendarroch means crag of oaks. This huge granite outcrop supports magnificent oak woodland, which is unusual in this part of Scotland. Several signposted paths ascend the wooded slopes from where there are fine views over Ballater, nestling below, and to Mount Keen and the peaks above Glen Muick.

Old Royal Station, Ballater

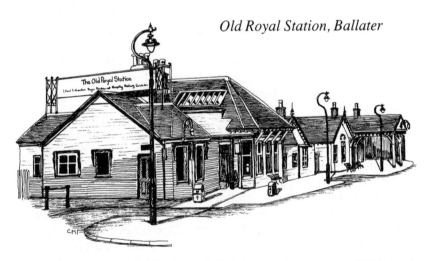

1. From the car park behind the church, cross the green by the church to the main street and turn left to Station Square. Continue up the main street, crossing over the now defunct railway line. There is pavement only on the left side of the road here, but when it starts on the right side, cross with care. Walk on past a converted church, on the left, to a street on the right, signed 'Craigendarroch Walks', where you turn right.

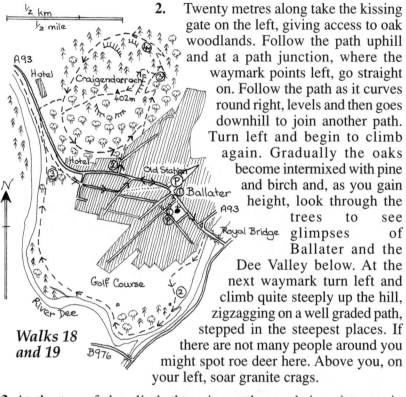

½ km
½ mile

A93
Hotel
Craigendarroch
402m
Hotel
Old Station
Ballater
A93
Royal Bridge
Golf Course
N
River Dee
Walks 18 and 19
B976

2. Twenty metres along take the kissing gate on the left, giving access to oak woodlands. Follow the path uphill and at a path junction, where the waymark points left, go straight on. Follow the path as it curves round right, levels and then goes downhill to join another path. Turn left and begin to climb again. Gradually the oaks become intermixed with pine and birch and, as you gain height, look through the trees to see glimpses of Ballater and the Dee Valley below. At the next waymark turn left and climb quite steeply up the hill, zigzagging on a well graded path, stepped in the steepest places. If there are not many people around you might spot roe deer here. Above you, on your left, soar granite crags.

3. At the top of the climb there is another path junction, again waymarked with arrows pointing left and straight ahead. On a tree is a sign which says turn left to go to the top and straight ahead to go round the hill. This walk turns left and goes up above the trees where the ground is open and there are great slabs of granite. The view from the summit is splendid. Ballater appears laid out at your feet. When you can bear to leave this high spot, retrace your steps to the last waymark and turn left. The path zigzags downhill, quite steeply, through bilberry and woodrush, shadowed with birch and pine. Opposite, on the far side of the Pass of Ballater, is another steep crag, Creag an t-Seabhaig, which glows a glorious red in late afternoon sunshine. Through the pass runs a road, by-passing the village of Ballater. The pass was formed from a fault line in the granite cut out by glacial ice.

4. Continue along the narrow path high above the road of the pass almost hidden in the depths below you. Look in the trees for coal

72

Treecreeper

and great tits and you may see a tree creeper searching the trunks for tiny insects. Eventually the slopes, on either side of the path, becomes less precipitous, and the path runs along above a low wall. Oaks reappear and increase in frequency until they are the dominant tree again. Ignore the path going uphill on the left. Continue gently downhill, circling round the hill, until you reach the first waymark you met on entering the wood. Turn right here and go downhill to the gate and back into the street. Retrace your steps to the centre of Ballater.

Practicals

Type of walk: A delightful woodland walk to the top of the hill sheltering Ballater, from where there are spectacular views.

Distance: 2 miles/3.4km
Time: 1–2 hours
Maps: OS Explorer 388 or 405, OS Landranger 44

73

19

Ballater riverside walk

Leave your vehicle in Station Square car park, Ballater, grid ref 370958. See map on page 72 for this walk.

The attractive village of **Ballater** lies on a meander of the River Dee under the shelter of the striking wooded hill of Craigendarroch. Two hundred years ago mineral rich water was discovered at nearby Pannanich Wells, which resulted in the growth of the Ballater to cater for those who wished to take the 'waters'. Queen Victoria and her descendants used the rail line to Ballater on their way to Balmoral, regularly, until it closed in 1966 after exactly a century of use. The trackbed is now a walkway and cycle-path.

Royal Bridge, Ballater

The **River Dee** rises at springs, the Wells of Dee, on the immense Braeriach plateau just east of Einich Cairn, at about 4026 ft/1220m above sea level. Its start is spectacular. It falls 495 ft/150m over the lip of the great corrie of Braeriach (An Garbh Choire). It rushes on under several bridges, down waterfalls and cascades for many long miles before reaching Royal Deeside passing through Braemar and Ballater on its way to the sea at Aberdeen. For much of the latter part it is accompanied by the A93 and the now defunct railway line. It is a great salmon river.

Caledonian pine forest

C.M. Isherwood

1. Leave Ballater's station square in a south-easterly direction. Walk on along the A93, with the village's fine church to your right. Go on along Bridge Street to come to Ballater Bridge. Descend the waymarked steps, to the right of the bridge, to the path beside the Dee. Turn right and walk upstream, keeping a look out for dippers bobbing on rocks in or close to the water. Trees line the bank of the wide, surging, peat stained river. Go through a gate where a sign welcomes walkers and on through the next gate to continue along a wide track in front of houses. Pass beside a caravan site and, at the Y-junction, take the left branch.

75

2. Go on the signposted footpath that runs between the golf course and the river. Here you should watch out for golf balls. Then the path drifts away from the links and goes on beside alders. On either side of the way heather and birch scrub flourish. The path then comes close beside the golf course again. From here you can see the fine mountain, Lochnagar. Continue on the pleasing way beside the lovely Dee to reach a car park, with picnic tables set among trees.

3. Turn right to walk through the trees and then join Old Line Road and then Dundarroch Road. Continue left up Invercauld Road to the A93. Here walk right to return to the village.

Black grouse

Practicals

Type of walk: Short and attractive, with fine open views of the surrounding hills, skirting a golf course and following the banks of the Dee.

Distance:	2 miles/3.2km
Time:	1 ½ hours
Maps:	OS Explorer 388, OS Landranger 44

20

Cambus o' May and Muir of Dinnet

Park in the Forest Enterprise car park at Cambus o' May, grid ref 404981. Access to this parking area is from the A93 2 ½ miles, east, from Ballater.

The **Muir of Dinnet**, a national nature reserve, lies 6 ¼ miles east of Ballater. Mixed birch and pine have spread naturally since the 1940s and among the trees you might spot red squirrels. In winter watch out for large flocks of greylag geese flying overhead from their roost on the nearby shallow lochs of Kinord and Davan. Otters use the lochs, bogs and marshes. The moorland part of the reserve supports heather and bearberry.

The Allt na Dabhaich rises on the slopes of Culblean hill, north-east of Ballater, and then descends through a steep rocky gorge.

In the Vat

The burn then tumbles in a fine little waterfall into the **Vat**. The Vat is a huge pothole in the granite, with very smooth sides. It looks like a collapsed cave. It gives its name to the tumbling water and is called Vat Burn, or Burn o'Vat, on the OS map. It is one of Scotland's famous natural curiosities.

Walk 20

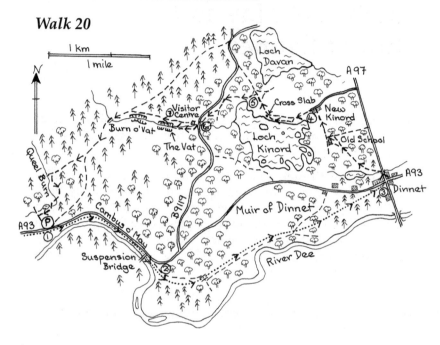

1. Return to the A93 down the entrance track to the car park and cross with care. Go through a small gate almost opposite, which gives access to the old Deeside railway track, now a walkway and cycle track. Turn left and enjoy strolling the old track, which is attractively lined with birch trees, and with the River Dee down below to your right, where you might spot dippers and common sandpipers. After 1 ¼ miles the elegant white suspension bridge at Cambus o'May comes into view, and then the track goes past the footbridge and on by the old station.

2. Here the track diverges from both the main road and the river to run midway between them across the Muir of Dinnet. At first the pines on your right are dense and appear to have been planted but soon they become scattered and interspersed with birch; the woodland to your left is mainly birch. Cross a wooden bridge over

a vehicle track, which then divides and one branch runs parallel to the pathway you are on. The birches on the left come to an end and you continue over open heather moorland, colourful and sweet smelling in August, with a scattering of fine pine trees. Pause to look behind for

Goldeneyes

splendid views up Deeside to the higher hills. Cross the vehicle track again, at a level crossing this time, and continue through pines to the village of Dinnet, where you leave the old railway track by a bicycle gap and cross the A93 again. There is a pub here—the Loch Kinord.

3. Walk east for a few metres to the crossroads and turn left onto the A97, fortunately a much quieter road than the A93. Use the pavement on the right. Beyond the last house, the A-road crosses a small burn. Almost immediately, beyond the bridge, take a gate on the left and follow the small path into birch and pine woodland. There is an information board about the national nature reserve and a map. Continue through the open woodland past a lochan on your left. The pine trees disappear and the woodland becomes increasingly birch. At an indistinct Y-junction take the right branch—this is the less obvious path—and follow it until you can turn left on to a track. Go through a gate and continue past an old schoolhouse, set about with pine trees, to a track junction. Turn right and walk downhill to go through a gate, which you are reminded to 'close and fasten or else it will be locked'. The track goes up the left side of two fields, the second one having a fine row of sycamore, beech and thorn trees edging it. At the top go past a barn to emerge onto a paved road. This is New Kinord.

4. Turn left and walk past a house. The road immediately becomes a reinforced track. Go through the gate into woodland and then continue along the edge of a field. There is a splendid view to your left over Loch Kinord to the hills. Beyond a wall gap, turn left, following a green arrow waymark and walk down to the loch shore. In winter look for greylag geese, goldeneye and whooper swans.

Turn right at the next waymark and walk along the edge of the loch. Go through a small wooden gate and then turn right at the next waymark. The path goes uphill to an enclosure containing an unusual Pictish cross stone, carved as a Celtic cross. Continue on past the stone to join the grassy track you left to go down to the shore of the loch, and turn left along it.

5. At a Y-junction, with a waymark post, take the left fork, following red arrows and, 50 metres further on, turn left on a small path, following the red arrow. This path is delightful, winding up and down through hummocky glacial deposit landscapes. The head of Loch Kinord, surrounded by reeds, is to your left. The path goes along a narrow low ridge through birch and heather. Eventually you reach a car park just off the B9119, with a cairn and plaque commemorating the opening of the reserve for the Queen's silver jubilee. Cross the tarmac and take a tiny path at the far side, which leads, in a few metres, to a grassy track. Turn left. At the next red arrow turn right onto another path, then left onto a track and, immediately left, onto another path. This is all clearly waymarked and the effect of it all is to take you along more or less parallel with the B-road, bringing you out opposite the visitor centre at Burn o'Vat. Cross the road to the centre.

6. After studying the interesting displays, go on across the front of the building and down to the left of the toilet block, to turn right on a path going up the Burn o'Vat. Cross the burn on a wooden bridge. There is another bridge a little higher up the burn but do not cross this at the moment; instead carry on to the apparent end of the path, where the burn emerges from a cleft in the granite beyond which you can glimpse a

Whooper swans

80

waterfall. It is actually a double cleft, with most of the burn going through the left one and shallow water with stepping stones in the right one. With minimal scrambling make your way through the second cleft into 'the Vat', an amazing spherical pothole carved out by glacial meltwater and floored with red sand, with the burn flowing across it from the waterfall. It is a sight not to be missed. If you are feeling very energetic it is possible to scramble up beside the waterfall and make your way upstream along the gorge to its end, where you emerge in a heathery hollow from which you can easily rejoin the path. This walk, however, goes back through the cleft and returns to the bridge you ignored on your way upstream. Cross the bridge and climb the path on the far side, signed 'viewpoint'.

7. At a T-junction above the steep part of the valley, turn left. Follow this path as it winds through pine and birch above the Burn o'Vat, with occasional glimpses down into the gorge. Eventually the path joins a forest track, where you turn left. Walk down the grassy track, leaving the reserve and entering Forest Enterprise land. At a post with a yellow waymark, turn right along a good path which takes you into lovely mixed-age pine forest. Turn left at a red waymarked path just before the Queel Burn, where there is a granite slab seat. Go down the path as it winds round more hummocks and through more hollows. Turn right, following the waymark at the next junction, and continue onto a ridge running round a tiny lochan. At its outflow turn left onto another path and then shortly left again. This path brings you down to the car park.

Practicals

Type of walk: This is a great walk along the trackbed of an old railway, through fine woodland, over colourful (in season) moorland and with several archaeological and natural—especially glacial—phenomena.

Distance:	9 ½ miles/15.4km
Time:	4–5 hours
Maps:	OS Explorer 405, OS Landranger 37 and mostly on 44 as well.

21

Logie Coldstone

Park tidily at the end of an unsigned track, grid ref, 428039, just beyond Bridgend cottage, on the left. To reach this leave the A93 between Aboyne and Ballater, at Dinnet cross roads. Proceed north towards Strathdon for 3.9 miles. Turn left at a signpost for Groddie (no through road). Continue for 0.4 miles.

Red squirrels are diurnal, with peaks of activity at dawn and before dusk. In former times it was greatly persecuted, squirrel hunts being a popular pastime. Groups of men and youths would stone the animal from tree to tree until they had forced it into one that stood alone. There it was stoned, until it dropped to the ground trying to escape, where it succumbed under a shower of more stones. Today it is greatly protected. Special feeding boxes are placed in woodland where only the red squirrel and not the larger grey can obtain the food. Rope ladders, with feeding boxes at both ends, are strung high between trees so that the reds can get to trees on both sides of a busy road where it passes through woodland. Grey squirrels have been seen in Lower Deeside but the red is still holding its own in the pine woods of Upper Deeside and is indeed common here still.

Forest path near Allalogie

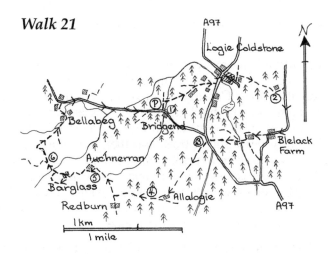

Walk 21

1. Walk up the unmade road and take the right branch where the road divides. Continue on through open woodland, with grassy clearings. Watch out for red squirrels, jays, great spotted woodpeckers and roe deer. Ignore a left turn and carry on to turn left onto the A97 to walk into the tiny village of Logie Coldstone. Bear right just beyond a building on the right, once a church and now a private dwelling, and carry on until you have passed two pretty original cottages on your left. Here turn left to walk in front of two new bungalows on your right, along an obvious track. Beyond the second bungalow bear right to walk a sandy track which heads into pleasing birch and conifer woodland. Carry on where the path takes you deeper into mainly conifer woodland.

2. Emerge from the trees, with pasture land to the right. At the end of the track, turn right to walk a narrow metalled lane and follow it where it bears right to Blelack farm. Where the road swings sharp left beyond the farmhouse, carry on ahead to pass the five-storey Blelack House (1881). Just beyond bear left, ignore the entrance track to the house and turn right to cross the footbridge over a small burn. Go on to pass close beside a cottage on the left, ignoring the track going right, and press on ahead on a track through mixed woodland to reach the A97.

3. Cross and take the track opposite through pine woodland, with heather and bilberry below. Here you might see tree creepers and more roe deer. Continue to pass two derelict buildings with corrugated roofs, named Allalogie on the map. Follow the path as it joins another (both indistinct here) and wind right to cross a ditch.

4. Head on through more open birch woodland, where the way becomes delightfully hillocky, with the Corbett, Morven, seemingly just across the valley. Continue through a tied hurdle and on along the pleasing track, with birch trees lying back from the path. Pass the remnants of an old croft and follow the now faint track as it winds, slightly left through trees and then across a grassy area, with a wall away to your left and a cottage named Redburn, beyond the wall. A few yards on you join a clear track where you turn right now with Morven on your left and a wide extensive view, to your right, over the lowlands of Cromar. Carry on over a wide open area which was probably well settled once.

5. Follow the track to the next cottage, which has lots of sheds beyond it. Here bear left before the gate and wind round to the left of the house (Auchnerran) to rejoin the track beyond the curtilage. Press on along the good track and head uphill in the direction of another cottage, named Barglass. The main track here goes past the cottage and across the field beyond it. If there are young bullocks in the field they may chase after you and you may prefer to go round the outside. To do this pass some ruined outbuildings and bear left, away from the main track, beside a wall on your right. Go on ahead for a few steps on the track and then climb gently, and diagonally

Rockroses

84

right, to a gate through the fence. Keep to the left of the field boundary to the far corner where you wind right beside the fence and carry on to a gate on your right where you rejoin the main track. Do not pass through but follow the track left, towards Morven, with a plantation to your right.

6. After a hundred metres leave the good track and walk right on a tiny path on the slope of a hillock, well above a wide boggy section on the right. Continue on the improving path and keep parallel with, but well away from, the fence on the right and go on along the slope. Wind left round the next hillock on a faint path and then go on to pass to the right of the next hillock. Look here for the pretty rock rose flowering in the short grass. Then the faint path heads towards another hillock, keeping left of it as it descends to a gate onto a good farm track, with a large bog to your left. Press on and keep left on the major track, ignoring the access track to Bellabeag. Carry on to a narrow road, where you turn right. Walk on along the quiet road for a mile to rejoin your car.

Red squirrel

Practicals

Type of walk: A generally level walk on tracks and paths through woodland, across open country and along virtually traffic free lanes. A delightful rural walk.

Distance: 5 ½ miles/9km
Time: 3 hours
Maps: OS Explorer 405, OS Landranger 37

22

Aboyne

Park in the square in front of the old station at Aboyne, grid ref 529987.

Aboyne lies on the A93 half way between Banchory and Ballater. It is located on the north bank of the River Dee. Before 1800 there was some sort of village here. The turning point came in 1828 with the building of a bridge across the Dee. The Deeside railway reached Aboyne from Banchory in 1859, replacing the coach service that had run twice daily, eastwards. The railway was extended to Ballater in 1866. In 1966 the railway was closed as part of the 'Beeching cuts'. Recently its pleasing railway station was converted to an attractive range of shops. Aboyne is a busy place in high season, but with its large open area next to the A93 it never seems too crowded.

Belwade farm is one of the centres of the **International League for the protection of horses**, ponies, donkeys and mules. It runs five centres dedicated to the recovery and rehabilitation of these animals. These centres are not sanctuaries but places

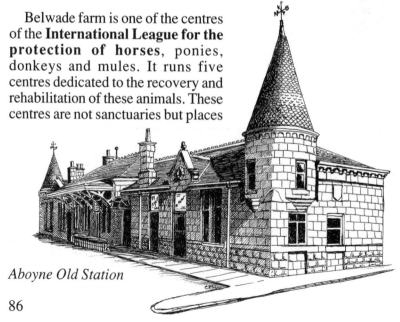

Aboyne Old Station

where each animal can receive care to return them to full health and then place them in a well-matched and loving new home. If you are interested in the many activities that place here, make yourself known to a member of staff to find out what is going on—perhaps you might see a shoeing competition.

Walk 22

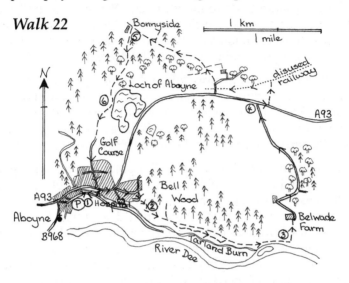

1. With your back to the old station building, cross the square to the far right corner and carry on along the road to the end of the houses. Stroll the continuing narrow lane until you reach a sturdy footbridge over the Tarland Burn, which you cross. Climb the railed path to join the A93 and walk right. After a very short distance, where the A-road begins to bear left, take a slip road on the right. Walk ahead to where the road bears right down to the hospital, and here press on ahead along Bellwood Drive. Then turn right to walk Old Town Road, watching for the entrance, on the left, into the pleasing deciduous Bell Wood. Ignore any paths going off left or right and carry on ahead along the main track.

2. Follow the track as it swings right and bear left at a T-junction. Go over a stile, ignoring a left turn before it and one after it. Stroll on through lofty pines. Join the wide track coming in on your left to walk on ahead and soon afterwards take a narrow path, on the right, with glimpses through the trees of the River Dee. Follow this for half a mile and then turn left along the edge of the wood to pass through a gap in a wall and leave the woodland by a stile over a fence on the right. Walk ahead and then drop down a slope and carry on along a grassy swathe that winds round the corner of a fence and then goes ahead as a long straight fenced grassy track. To your right alder carr thrives about the Tarland Burn. To the left are fenced pastures where horses graze. You may be tempted to descend concrete steps, on the right, to the side of the tributary very close to where it joins the Dee. Alas you cannot reach the side of the Dee but you might spot several dippers.

3. Go with the track as it turns left and climbs gently to Belwade farm, one of the centres of the international league for the protection of horses. There is a shop here and a visitor centre. Bear left over the metalled way and then go on to walk for a mile and three quarters along the narrow access lane through the lovely countryside.

4. On reaching the A93, cross and walk right, using the wide grassy verge. Beyond the first house, take a track on the left to descend and then ascend towards a house, West Roseburn. Just before the house, wind left to walk the tree-lined dismantled Aberdeen to Ballater railway track as it moves deep into the Deeside countryside. On reaching a road turn right and walk on for a short distance. Where the road winds right and a track goes off left, go ahead to a locked gate, signed Bonnyside. Climb the gate and stroll on, steadily climbing the delightful track through gorse, bracken and scattered birch. Press on and before the next locked gate note the 'diversion'

signed path, on the right, which provides an alternative route if the herd of cattle in the next pasture seem too daunting. If not, climb the gate, and continue on along the upper track until you approach the ruins of Bonnyside.

Dipper

5. Descend the pasture, left, before the ruins and walk ahead to climb another locked gate into pleasing woodland of open birch and pine. Ignore a right turn and, at a Y-junction, go on ahead where the path narrows. The way continues through an opening in the fence and then moves into denser pine woodland. The way through the trees is clear and very soon you emerge through another gap in the fence. Ahead is a fine view of Loch of Aboyne, with the manicured greens of Aboyne golf course to your left. Descend steadily along a pleasant path through bracken to come to the side of the loch, where aquatic bistort flowers.

6. Climb the sturdy wooden stile on the right and, beyond, walk left along the side of the golf course. Follow the track as it winds downhill, keeping to the right of the club house to walk down Golf Road to the side of the A93. Cross, with care, turn left and in a few steps walk right to descend the railed steps to the footbridge over the burn, taken earlier. Turn right and continue ahead to reach the parking area at the Old Station, with time left perhaps to explore Aboyne.

Aquatic bistort

Practicals

Type of walk: This route takes you through pine woodland, over pastures, along a trackbed of a railway and beside a pretty loch—great for all the family.

Distance: 6 miles/9.8km
Time: 3–4 hours
Maps: OS Explorer 405, OS Landranger 37

23

Glen Tanar and the Fungle Road

Park in the pay-and-display car park on the right of the road at Braeloine, grid ref 479966. This is reached by a minor road off the B976 about 1 ¼ miles/2km west of Aboyne, on the south side of the Dee. The turning up to Glen Tanar is flanked by stone gateposts and is rather imposing. Drive into the glen for a further 1 ½ miles.

The **Mounth Roads** included the Monega Pass, Jock's Road, Capel Mounth, the Mounth Keen, the Firmounth Road and the Fungle Road. These were used by travellers, pedlars and illegal whisky travellers on their journeys from Deeside, over the Mounth—a long rolling line of hills—to the lowlands of Angus and the Tay. The area around the church in Glen Tanar is the site of the township of Braeloine, which used to serve the traffic on the Firmounth Road. There was an inn, several shoemakers' shops—very necessary when all traffic was on foot—and about 15 houses. By the end of the 19th century the travellers had all gone and the village was in ruins because people went by different ways, society changed, the railways came to Deeside and there were 'proper' roads.

The Seat

The **Glen Tanar estate** was bought by William Cunliffe-Brooks in the 1860s. He came from Manchester and was an eccentric banker and a MP. He built the pleasing simple church for the estate and its workers and generally improved the estate especially for deer and grouse shooting. The area is administered by the Glen Tanar Charitable Trust who operate a ranger service from the Braeloine visitor centre, telephone 013398 86072.

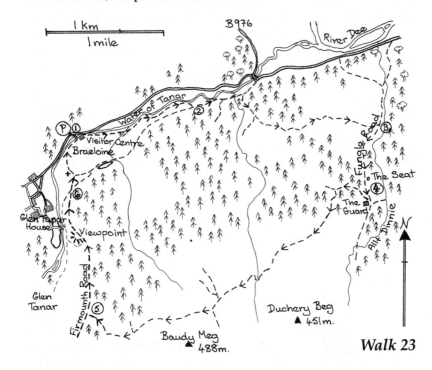

Walk 23

1. Return to the entrance to the car park and cross the road. Go over a fine arched stone bridge and turn left towards Braeloine visitor centre. Walk round the back of the centre, go past the toilets and climb the stile in the corner of the fence. Follow the continuing path across grass and into woodland. The delightful way goes on along beside the Water of Tanar, which flows clear and fast through tree-lined banks. On the tiny sandy 'beaches' look for otter footprints. Watch out, too, for dippers, herons and long tailed tits. After a quarter of a mile, cross a stile, turn right and cross another. Then go over a bridge across a little burn. Turn left, cross another stile and another bridge and go up the slope to walk above the river.

There are fields on your right which eventually come to an end and are replaced by young trees. Then the path comes down to just above the river again. Go on to the end of the young plantation and follow the fence round right and up a bank to join a forest track.

2. Turn left and walk the track, ignoring the first track which goes off right. Enjoy the fine view down to a bend in the river, which here is full of rapids. Cross a bridge over a tributary, the Allt Roy, and take the next track right, leading uphill through a few mature pines. Carry on into a valley which has been recently replanted with young conifers. At a Y-junction take the left branch, continuing to climb left of the new plantings which have orange netting on their fence so that capercaillies see them and don't fly into them. Here you might spot siskins and crossbills. Press on uphill past an area where young broadleaved trees have been planted and wind round left above it to continue to a col at the top of the track. Descend on the far side through open pine and then moorland, with a splendid view over Aboyne to the hills beyond. Continue where the path contours and then comes down as a cutting, with steep banks on both sides, to a gate with a stile beside it.

3. Beyond, turn right to walk the Fungle Road, one of the ancient Mounth paths. The path climbs and higher up passes between steep banks covered in woodrush, fern, moss and lichen-hung larch. On

Crossbill

the left near the top of the hill is a seat, which is marked on the map. It is a low wall of flat stones forming ¼ of the circumference of a circle, with a platform in front. The entrance is formed by two large carved boulders. The left one has a pattern and the dates, 1860–1900, and on the other face, the words, 'O Ye Mountains O Ye Waters Praise Ye the Lord'. The right one says, 'Rest and be Thankful'. There must have been a wonderful view from here at one time but it is now partly obscured by trees: however it is a lovely place to eat your picnic!

92

4. Continue climbing gently to a cottage, The Guard, where several tracks and paths cross. Turn sharply right and go through a gate into Glen Tanar forest, where a sign welcomes walkers. The track soon curves left and goes through mature pines. At the next junction, just as the track begins to go downhill, turn left. After a short climb the track levels and emerges from the trees onto open heather moor. Follow it where it contours below the hilltop but remains high above the valley. Ford a burn, ignore a track right and then another on the left and go on round the hillside, an unremarkable rounded hump which rejoices in the name of Baudy Meg! From here are fine and ever widening views of the Mounth and the Deeside hills. Go ahead at the next junction and then descend, quite steeply, a much rougher way into Glen Tanar.

5. Turn right onto a level track, the Firmounth road, another of the old Mounth roads. Ahead and slightly left is Glen Tanar House among trees and with a loch in front. Carry on along the track as it crosses an open space and then by larches on the right and scattered pines to the left. After half a mile and where another track joins the one you are on, from the left, you reach a fenced viewpoint with seats and a view indicator. From here you can see Upper Glen Tanar spread before you, full of splendid pines, with the river gleaming in the valley flats and the high moors of the Mounth at the back. Perhaps this is the place for a second picnic.

6. Go on along the Firmounth Road, with trees on either side, to pass through a gate. Beyond, go ahead at the cross of tracks to walk along the edge of the enclosure round the small church and turn left over a cattle grid at the end. If you wish to visit the church, take the stile into the precincts. Then continue along the track to the bridge by the visitor centre and so back to the car park.

Practicals

Type of walk: A good walk through woodlands and over high heather slopes on paths and tracks, with splendid views.

Distance: 8 miles/13km
Time: 4–5 hours
Maps: OS Explorer 395, OS Landranger 44

24

Scolty Hill

Park in the car park among the trees of Blackhall Forest, grid ref 687948, close to Auchattie. To reach this leave Banchory by the Fettercairn Road, cross the River Dee and after a ¼ of a mile, take an acute right turn, signposted Scolty Hill and Auchattie. Go on to take a right-angled left and then go on straight ahead. It is all well signposted.

The delightful mainly tree-girt **Scolty Hill** supports a very tall monument on its flat grassy summit. On the latter are two toposcopes to help you identify the hills around, and also a trig point. Several waymarked routes take you to the summit and you can choose your route, up and down, making use of the map on the information board at the start of the walk.

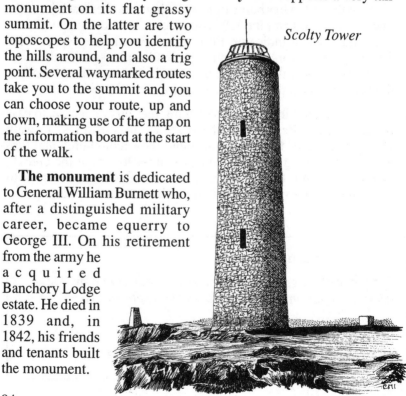

Scolty Tower

The monument is dedicated to General William Burnett who, after a distinguished military career, became equerry to George III. On his retirement from the army he acquired Banchory Lodge estate. He died in 1839 and, in 1842, his friends and tenants built the monument.

Walk 24

1. Leave by the exit route from the car park and turn left to pass the information board. Just beyond, walk left along a delightful path, through trees, which is waymarked with red and yellow banded posts. Join a wider track where you carry on, right, and continue to the edge of the trees. Here follow the track, right, with a pasture to the left and trees to the right. Soon the path leads into forestry again and begins to climb gently. Turn right as directed by the waymark and then left at a Y-junction along a narrower way through mature and rather majestic spruce. Go on through a kissing gate to walk the ongoing grassy track.

2. At the next marker post, look on the far side of the post for the white arrow, directing you left up a slope. Carry on up the bouldery path as it climbs steadily along the pleasing way, passing through birch and larch. Then the way winds right and climbs steeply, still with the forest to your left. Ascend through boulders and great cushions of heather, to come to the wide grassy plateau and the foot of the towering monument. Here you might be tempted to climb the winding staircase, within the monument, for an even more extensive view of the glorious countryside.

3. Cross the plateau and by the trig point look for the several ways off the top. Ignore the white waymarked track on your right and

95

also ignore the track to your left. Take the grassy track which continues along the ridge and leaves the plateau between the two paths described above. A short distance along, take the right fork to a minor summit, through the vast dome of heather. The way, a joy to walk, soon becomes wider and grassy, and descends gently. It brings you to the foot of the slope and a wide grassy track, where you turn right to continue. At a Y-junction take the left branch and go on down to join another grassy track. Turn right again and stroll the pleasing terraced way below birch, enjoying as you go the view down into the glen on your left.

4. Just before the kissing gate, turn left and follow the red marked post. The track, another delight, edges the forest on the right and there are scattered birches to your left, where roe deer linger. Go through the next kissing gate and walk on. At a T-junction turn right onto a forest road and in a few steps, right again at the next T-junction. Follow this way as it winds round right as directed by a post with a red arrow and a red footprint on it.

5. Then at a branching of tracks take the next waymarked left turn, along another forest road. Watch out for the red arrow directing you right up a path, through the forest, close to a ruined lichened wall on the left. At the boundary wall ahead, turn left before it and immediately go through a purpose made gap in the wall. Walk ahead on a narrow path. At a cross of tracks, wind left and remain on this path as it winds right and continues up a slope. Join the forest road and turn left to return to the parking area.

Practicals

Type of walk: This is a most satisfactory walk. It takes you steadily uphill through delightful woodland, full of bird song, onto a plateau from where the views are spectacular. The return through a different part of the forest is equally pleasing.

Distance: 4 miles/6.5km
Time: 2 hours
Maps: OS Explorer 406, OS Landranger 45

25

Hill of Fare

Park in the grounds of Raemoir House Hotel, grid ref 695996, but remember not to obstruct access to any of the buildings. The hotel welcomes walkers but asks that they let the reception desk know that they are leaving a car in the grounds. The hotel is reached by a tree-lined drive off the A980 at its jnction with the B977, 2 ½ miles north of Banchory.

The Hill of Fare, a forested ridge running from east to west, has four summits—Craigrath, Blackyduds, Greymore and Meikle Tap. Sitka spruce, larch and Scots pine, found on the lower slopes of the Hill, thrive in the once boggy land about the Burn of Corriche. Above the forest the moorland, clad in a vast expanse of heather, is glorious in high summer. On your walk look in the forest for pine martens, red squirrels, siskins, crossbills, coal tits and bullfinches. Over the high moor you should see grouse and meadow pipits.

The battle of Corriche took place about the head of the Corriche Burn on October 28, 1562 between the forces of Mary, Queen of Scots and the Earl of Huntly. The Queen's forces were victorious and the Earl of Huntly died of a stroke on

Corrichie Monument

the battleground. In 1951 the Deeside Field Club erected a 12 ft high granite monument to the battle, 3 miles east of Raemoir. The Gaelic inscription says:

Cuimhnichibh la Coire Fhrasichdh
which translates as
Remember the day of Corriche.

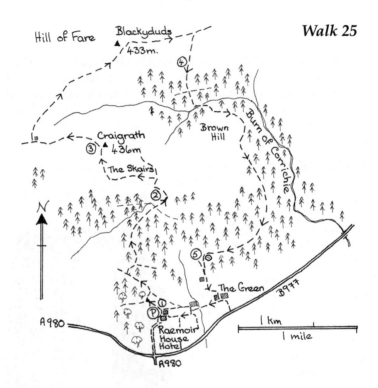

Walk 25

1. From the hotel set off towards the Hill of Fare, passing left of the Ha house beyond. The Ha is believed to have been built in 1715. It is a hall-house, a more comfortable dwelling than the castellated tower houses lived in by earlier lairds. It is a listed building and is now the hotel annexe. Bear left to climb a good track into the conifers of Spy Brae wood. At the T-junction turn right. Go on through a gate and then follow the track as it passes through larch where you might spot crossbills. Carry on past a hut and, at the next T-junction, just before the edge of the wood, bear right to walk through Craigbeg Wood. Continue on, up and up, to turn left at the next T-junction, where the path levels and the way is littered with pine needles and cones shredded by squirrels and where you might spot a pine marten.

2. Emerge from the trees onto slopes clad with bracken, heather and rush. At the next junction of paths go straight ahead to follow the path as it winds left, steadily climbing, through a sea of heather

Pine marten

with, between, bright green patches of bilberry. Pause as you go to look, left, across the valley to see row after row of hills and the River Dee, silvery, in the valley bottom. Follow the main track as it bears right and then take a left fork to walk on the terraced way below crags (the Skairs), with the land, to the left, sloping steeply down. Curve right to come to the imperceptible summit of Craigrath, 1311 ft/435m, a tiny mound marked with a small pile of stones.

3. Continue on the now descending track to reach a sturdy bothy. Just beyond, follow the track which turns right through the vast sea of heather. From here you can soon glimpse, right, the tree clad slopes about the Burn of Corriche. Press on to the brow of the next slope and then descend easily to the col below. At the point where the track is again about to climb steeply, take the wide rough track going off right, where you should take care on your descent.

4. As you come level with a small picturesque roofless ruin, where a solitary rowan and a pine grow, you might decide this is the place for your first break. Then drop down into the trees of the Howe of Corriche, where the track rapidly improves. Ignore the grassy trod coming in on the left, and go on down to follow the track, over a burn, and bear left. Then climb slightly, with the trees of the forest to the left and the open heather slopes of Brown Hill to the right. Press on along the track for nearly a mile, round Brown Hill, to reach the pleasingly landscaped site of the old Raemoir Quarry.

5. Pass the old gunpowder hut and, leaving the trees behind, walk the track through fields and then the outbuildings of Green farm. Once past the farmhouse, turn right to stroll a wide hedged track, with forest trees on either side. At the Home farm bear left to join a another track, shadowed by trees, and carry on right. On joining a third track, stride ahead to come to the hotel.

Siskin

Practicals

Type of walk: A very satisfactory walk of contrasts. Choose a good day to climb through the forest onto the high heather moorland. The return is made through more woodland and then farmland. Easy to walk landrover tracks for much of the way.

Distance: 7 miles/11.4km
Time: 3–4 hours
Maps: OS Explorer 406, OS Landranger 38

26

Banchory to Crathes Castle

Leave your car in the George V Park, grid ref 697955. To reach this turn off the A93, as it passes through Banchory, into Dee Street, signposted for Fettercairn. Go past the pay and display car park (where there are toilets) and turn left into the large attractive park where there are parking bays between the trees.

The 16th century **Crathes Castle**, one of Scotland's finest baronial castles, has dramatic turrets, corbelling and crow step gables. Inside are remarkable painted ceilings and outside a famous walled garden. It was built for the Alexander de Burnard (now Burnett) of Leys and remained in the ownership of the family until it was gifted to the National Trust for Scotland (NTS). For

Crathes Castle

information on opening times tel: 01330 844525. The gardens and grounds, through which this walk passes, are open all year round from 9 am to sunset.

Walk 26

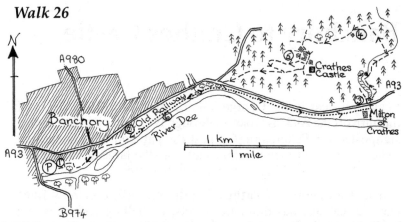

1. Walk on from the parking area along the continuing road, lined with forest trees, with the grounds of the spacious public park on either side. Go ahead at the cross of tracks, keeping dwellings to the right. Follow the track as it continues on and then winds right, with houses to the left. Bear left, still on the track, to pass an entrance to the Banchory Lodge Hotel. At the second entrance turn left and almost immediately pass through a gap in the fence on your right. Walk right along the continuing tarmac footpath at the back of a housing estate to come beside, on your right, the delightful River Dee, wide and surging. Continue through a little park and walk on through wild cherry trees, where in spring the bullfinches delight in the buds.

2. Carry on along the hedged track, which was once the bed of the Deeside Line from Aberdeen to Ballater. As soon as you spot a parallel path beside the River Dee, leave the railway bed and stroll on the delectable way beneath fine trees beside the river where fishermen cast for salmon. When your way is barred by a burn in a gully, bear left up steps, to rejoin the track and cross a picturesque bridge. Rejoin the riverside path as soon as you can. Eventually, at the farm and houses at Birenbaud, you have to walk, left, along a lane to rejoin the railway track. Turn right to continue, sometimes close to the A93, until you reach the entrance to the craft village of Milton of Crathes, where there is a restaurant, shop and gallery.

3. Here cross the busy A93 and walk on for a few steps to turn left into the access road to Crathes Castle. Pass through the iron gates and ignore the old road on the right. A few steps along take, on the right, the path waymarked with a red arrow. Head towards the mill pond, turn right and go over a rustic bridge. Walk left and then climb an arrowed slope to continue round a waymarked fenced area, where conifers have been removed and replanting is taking place (at the time of writing). The waymarks lead you to a footbridge over the Coy burn and then on a boardwalk over boggy ground. Carry on through woodland beside the chuckling burn. Turn right before the next footbridge and, with the stream to your left, go on through the forest. Cross the next footbridge and head on through conifers, soon with pastures to the left. Go over a little stone bridge across a dry gully and continue on a terraced path along the side of the forest.

4. At an old barn the route continues along a walled way parallel with a forest road. From now on the waymarks keep you first on one side of the road and then the other until eventually you have to re-join the road. Go on past a delightful adventure playground, on the left, to walk the road as it passes through trees and winds left between the outbuildings of the castle estate. To your left is the Horse Mill restaurant and then the toilets. To your right is the NTS shop. Between the two is a dramatic view of the fine castle.

5. Then leave the cluster of buildings and follow the pink and green waymarks out past an old ice house to climb to the viewpoint overlooking the forest. Go on from here following blue waymarks and bear steadily left to descend a natural granite stepped path to join a track below. Turn left and walk on to wind right before a small gate. The path leads you to an access drive, where you turn right to walk through more fine trees to the West Lodge and the A93. Cross the road and walk the verge, left, for a very short distance to a short section of old road. Drop down the bank to join a short reinforced track onto old railway bed once more. Turn right and retrace most of your outward route to Banchory.

Salmon leaping

103

6. Just before a hut, on the riverbank, descend left to drop down steps to the edge of the water. Then carry on along a railed raised way, that takes you high above the water, the walkway hugging the side of a very high granite retaining wall, with glorious views of the Dee. Here you might see salmon leaping, grey wagtails flitting downstream and herons waiting patiently for a catch. This walkway is a delight and should not be missed. At its end, climb the steps to the railway track and walk on to the gap in the fence taken earlier. Then retrace your steps to the parking area.

Wood anemones

Practicals

Type of walk: A level linear walk along the old railway bed and beside the River Dee. The walk through the grounds of Crathes Castle is a joy, with a short climb and descent from the viewpoint.

Distance: 7 miles/11.4km
Time: 3–4 hours
Terrain: Easy walking all the way.
Maps: OS Explorer 406, OS Landranger 38 or 45

27

Dunnottar Castle and Woods near Stonehaven

Park in the free Pier car park, grid ref 877856, overlooking the sea, at the south end of Stonehaven, where there are toilets.

Dunnottar Castle, the famous and magnificently sited stronghold of the Keiths, is a lofty headland fortress south of Stonehaven. It was defended from invasion by a huge natural chasm. In 1297 William Wallace burnt the fortress with its English garrison alive, inside. The tower on the cliff edge, was built in the late 14th century by Sir William Keith. The Keiths were counsellors to the sovereign and Mary Queen of Scots and her son King James VI visited Dunnottar several times. In the civil war it was besieged by Montrose who burnt Stonehaven and all the surrounding lands. After the Jacobite rebellion of 1715 the Keiths forfeited the castle and it was dismantled.

Dunnottar Castle

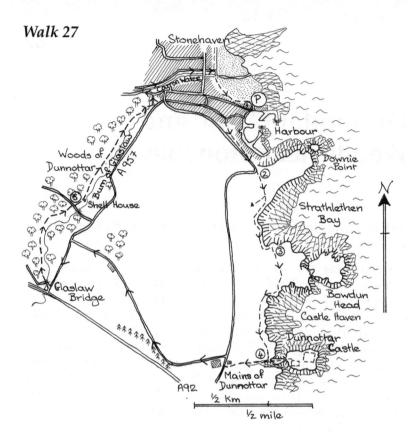

Walk 27

Stonehaven

Carron Water

P

Harbour

Woods of
Dunnottar

Burn of Glaslaw

A957

Downie
Point

Shell House

Strathlethen
Bay

Glaslaw
Bridge

Bowdun
Head
Castle Haven

Dunnottar
Castle

N

Mains of
Dunnottar

A92

½ Km

½ mile

1. Leave the car park by the exit to come to the edge of the small harbour. Bear right to pass Stonehaven's oldest building, the Tolbooth, used as a store during the construction of Dunnottar Castle. It now houses a museum and a restaurant. Continue, anticlockwise round the harbour-side, passing in front of some charming old buildings. Halfway round turn right up Wallace Wynd and then left up Castle Street. Carry on up a steep track and follow it as it winds left, climbing the sandstone hill which provides considerable shelter for the harbour below. Near the top is a seat and a toposcope. Continue on to join a narrow road and turn left. Walk on to where the road swings sharp right.

2. Here, take the fenced tarmacked footpath that continues ahead. It passes, on the right, a kissing gate that gives access to a tall sandstone monument, commemorating the dead of the 1914–18

106

war. The names of those who died in the 1939–45 war were later added to it. The construction has been left unfinished to remind people of the unfinished lives of the soldiers who died in the wars. There is a seat below the memorial, with a fine view over the town and the bay. Go on along the fenced path for a sudden first glimpse of the ruined castle, clinging precariously to its craggy lump above the open sea. When the fenced path reaches a stile, you are requested to keep dogs on the lead.

3. Walk on along the cliffs to climb an easy stile on the right. Cross a pasture and go on over two more stiles. Then a path, sometimes railed and always well maintained, takes you on along the edge of the high cliffs that rim Castle Haven. Pause to look back to the cliffs of conglomerate rock that jut into the bay, where fulmars nest. Wind on round the good path, high above the sea, where children and dogs should be under control at all times. The path then brings you to the long flight of concrete steps that leads down to a causeway on the narrow spine of rock by which the great mound is joined to the land. More steps lead up to the entrance to the castle, where you pay your entrance fee.

4. To continue the walk turn right at the top of the steps and stroll the wide track that leads to the castle's tiny car park and the narrow road, walked earlier. Cross, turn right and take the first left. Stride the steadily ascending metalled road, past a farm, to a right-angled corner. Then descend the quiet metalled road to reach the A957. Cross, with care, and turn left to walk the pavement towards the A92. Just before the A-road turn right, cross the bridge over the Burn of Glaslaw and right again into the Woods of Dunnottar at Glaslaw Gate (opening). From now on descend through fine woodland, using paths that keep close to the burn on your right. Look for Lady Kennedy's bath, a large stone circular trough through which flows the hurrying stream.

5. Cross a narrow road and continue on down through the lovely deciduous trees to visit Lady Kennedy's shell house. Peer through the iron grill to see the wonderfully decorated walls. This was built between 1800 and 1820 and, like the bath seen earlier, may have been built for her children's amusement—she had ten of them. Go on down to leave the woods by the Carron Gate. Walk ahead through a housing estate and then cross a fairly busy road. Turn left and almost immediately right to take the bridge over the Carron Water.

Turn right and continue to the busy Main Street. Cross and walk ahead, winding through buildings and private parking, to step onto the boardwalk along the bay. Turn right to return to the Pier car park.

Fulmar

Practicals

Type of walk: A dramatic cliff top walk to see the ruins of Dunnottar Castle. The return is made along mainly quiet roads and then a long, pleasing descent through deciduous woodland.

Distance: 4 ½ miles/7.25km
Time: 2 ½ hours
Maps: OS Explorer 396, OS Landranger 45

NB: The cliff top part of the walk should not be attempted in high winds.

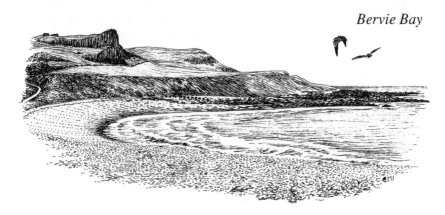

28

Inverbervie

Park in the beach car park at Inverbervie, grid ref 834723. To reach this leave the A92, which passes through the little town, by Kirkburn and follow it down to the shore.

Inverbervie stands on the western bank of a deep, narrow gorge through which the Bervie Water forced its way to the sea. Fishing continued from the shelter of the mouth of the river for almost 500 years, and harbour improvements were made by Thomas Telford in 1819. However by 1830 a shingle spit had grown across the mouth of the river, making access difficult for boats. Fishermen based in Inverbervie moved a mile or so down the coast to the better harbour at Gourdon.

Close to the south end of the Jubilee Bridge, at the northern end of the village, is the Hercules Linton Memorial. Hercules was born in Inverbervie and designed the *Cutty Sark* tea clipper, now moored at Greenwich in London. The memorial is in the form of a full size replica of the figurehead of the ship, the scantily clad witch Nannie from Robert Burns' poem 'Tam o' Shanter'.

Bervie Bay

After walking the track, known as Low Road, through the small fishing villages of Gourdon, Haughs Bay and Johnshaven, the return route is along the **Old Coach Road**, the main route for mail coaches for 200 years. As you near Inverbervie once more you pass the farmhouse, Sillyflatt, once an inn on the coach road.

Walk 28

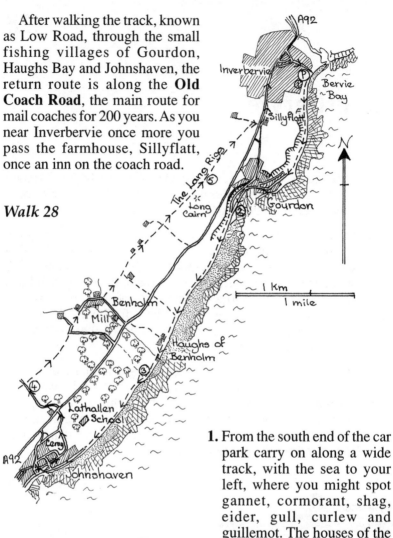

1. From the south end of the car park carry on along a wide track, with the sea to your left, where you might spot gannet, cormorant, shag, eider, gull, curlew and guillemot. The houses of the town are soon left behind and the track, once the bed of a railway line, continues ahead. Just beyond the gate over the track a narrow easier-to-walk path, nearer the sea, goes on parallel with the track. After a mile and a quarter you reach Gourdon, a fishing village, which clings limpet-like to steep slopes above it. Go past houses interspersed with fishing sheds to come to the sturdy harbour, overlooked by the Harbour Bar inn. Once a large seagoing fleet sailed out of the harbour but now the catch is mainly shellfish.

2. Wind round the harbour to join the waymarked coastal road, signposted Johnshaven. This soon becomes a track again and passes, in 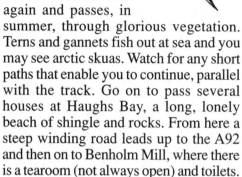 summer, through glorious vegetation. Terns and gannets fish out at sea and you may see arctic skuas. Watch for any short paths that enable you to continue, parallel with the track. Go on to pass several houses at Haughs Bay, a long, lonely beach of shingle and rocks. From here a steep winding road leads up to the A92 and then on to Benholm Mill, where there is a tearoom (not always open) and toilets.

Arctic skua chasing tern

This route could be used as a short cut if desired. Stroll on the level track, leaving the cliffs behind, with pastures stretching away to deciduous woodland. Among the trees you can see the turrets of Lathallen School.

3. Continue beside a wall, where another narrow path enables you to by-pass the track. Eventually the way becomes tarmacked and continues as Beach Road into Johnshaven. The large fishing village is strung out along a ledge between the A-road and the rocky beach. Carry on to the harbour from where

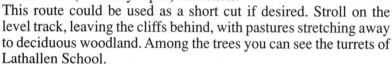

Terns

fishermen set off for crab and lobster. After a little exploration bear right with the road and right again in front of the Anchor Hotel. Then go left before the Church of Scotland and wind, right, round it. You are now three roads up from the coastal track and wending your way back north. Follow the road and carry on where it drops a little and then bears left and climbs steadily up a leafy walled road to pass the entrance to the school seen earlier. At the A-road turn right and walk the pavement for 300m. Cross the busy road and walk uphill on a road, signposted Fordoun and Laurencekirk.

4. Press on uphill to an electricity pole, numbered 15. Just beyond a narrow track, which has crossed the road, goes off right. In summer it can be overgrown but it is then a glorious floral way. Follow it until it reaches a road. Go ahead for a few steps and where the road winds left go on along the signposted track to drop downhill to rejoin the road again at some pretty cottages. Carry on to cross a burn and follow the road uphill, wind right through houses and swing left over another burn. Where the road swings right to descend to Benholm Mill, go ahead along the continuing coach road. (If you have shortened your walk and climbed up to the Mill, go on up to turn right to join the main walk here.) It is level to walk as it passes between pastures and then climbs steadily to Gourdon Hill, with its long cairn to your right.

5. The wide track, now known as Lang Rig, descends steadily over the fine pastures, with a wonderful view ahead of the cliffs around Bervie Brow beneath which snuggles Inverbervie. On joining an

Common Sandpiper

access track to a farm, turn right to the A92. Again cross with care, turn left, pass Sillyflatt and then drop down, a little to the right to walk the old road into the town. Turn right down Kirkburn to return to the car park.

Wood vetch

Practicals

Type of walk: A pleasing walk along a blustery coastline, with the return made high up on the hillside—equally blustery, with the possibility of a short cut.

Distance: Full walk 10 miles/16km. Leaving the coastal track at Benholm 7 miles/11km

Time: 4–5 hours/3–4 hours

Maps: OS Explorers 396 and 382, OS Landranger 45

29

St Cyrus

Park in the car park, grid ref 742635, opposite the small but delightful visitor centre, where there is a toilet block. St Cyrus lies six miles north of Montrose. To reach the parking area leave the A92 immediately north of the road bridge beside the fine viaduct, across the River North Esk, to turn right along a narrow lane, signposted 'Beach', and drive on for just over a mile.

The original village of **St Cyrus** developed around the river mouth of the North Esk but was engulfed by the sea during a cataclysmic storm in 1795. Today the village lies set back from the edge of the towering cliffs, which form such a magnificent backdrop to the National Nature Reserve.

The **high cliffs** of lava, set well back from the sea, are an ancient reminder of the original sea level before the end of the last ice age. The lowered sea level reflects the rising of the land after the release of the weight of ice, pressing down on it for thousands of years. The volcanic rock is rich in nutrients and so is home to many unusual plants.

St Cyrus

The **dunes** are very prominent at St Cyrus. The roots of spikey marram grass and grey-green sea lyme grass bind the sand and help in the formation of the dunes. Once the sand has been stabilised other plants can grow here.

Walk 29

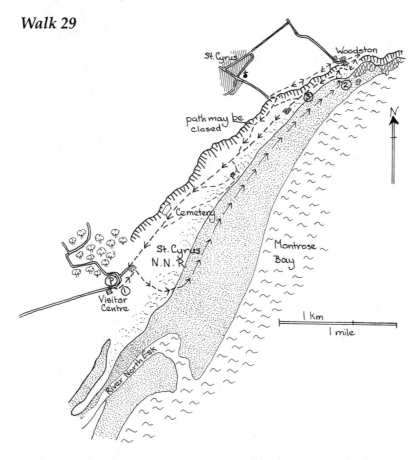

1. Leave the car park, join the railed way and walk left. Go on, right, along the boardwalk across the dune slacks where, in high summer, pink rest harrow and yellow bedstraw grow. As you climb through the dunes clustered bellflower adds to the mosaic of colour. Then descend to the beach, a wonderful curve of golden sand, stretching south to Montrose and north to Nether Woodston. Turn left and begin your stroll along the sands. Stretching out to sea from the beach are salmon fishing nets just as they have done ever since St Cyrus's 13th century charters. Offshore you might spot eiders and, later in the year, scoters and velvet scoters, the latter with bright white wing patches. To your left behind the dunes rear the spectacular lava cliffs.

Clustered Bellflower

2. As you approach several huge rocky outcrops, take the pleasing, waymarked, flower-lined path that climbs gently up the cliffs to the Woodston fishing station. Look for pale wood vetch on the cliff as you ascend. Follow the way as it winds left to join a reinforced track that passes between the fishing station and its outbuildings. Go on round with the track from where there is a marvellous view of the bay and its lighthouse at the far end. Carry on past a house and turn left to walk a delectable path along the cliff top, with lush vegetation on either side. Soon you can glimpse the spire of the church at St Cyrus. The delightful path leads to a small open area with three seats from where the views are stunning. Just beyond is a small car park and from it descend a few steps to a well placed seat. From here a path leads down the steep cliffs to the shore. At the time of writing this has been closed because of a landslip. If it has not been reopened when you do this walk, return along the cliff top to Woodston and go down the path taken earlier to the waymark at its foot.

3. Here walk a narrow sandy path, right, through the marram grass, passing under the steep cliffs. Go on the wider way behind a fishing station with its poles in place for drying the nets. On your right the track is joined by the paths that you might have used before the landslip. Look for fulmars nesting on the ledges of the cliffs and here you might spot a merlin hurtling across the way after some luckless prey. Eventually you arrive at the beautifully maintained Nether Kirkyard. The ancient name of the parish it served was Ecclesgreig and from this the name St Cyrus was derived. There

116

are some interesting plaques to be read in the burial ground. Beyond the kirk, pass a huge pasture of barley on the right and the dune slacks to the left as you return to the car park.

Common Scoters

Practicals

Type of walk: An exciting walk. In winter storms crash over the beach but on a warm summer's day it is idyllic for all the family.

Distance: 3–4 miles/ 5–6.5km depending on which path you take to return to the shore.
Time: 1–2 hours
Maps: OS Explorer 382, OS Landranger 45

Clachnaben and Hill of Edendocher

Park in the quarry car park, grid ref 648868, half a mile north of the Bridge of Dye, on the west side of the B974, the Old Military Road over Cairn of Mount.

The **Clachnaben Path Trust** is a wholly voluntary organisation, formed in 1997, by a group of people much concerned with the severe erosion of the footpath to the summit. Members repair and coordinate the work done on the path. As you progress towards the summit you will much appreciate their efforts.

Clachnaben (1900ft/585m) has a massive granite tor on its summit, which gives the hill its name, 'stone of the mountain', and makes it instantly recognisable from the surrounding countryside.

Clachnaben summit

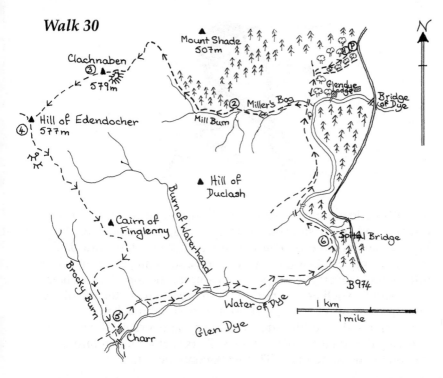

Clachnaben
③ ▲ 579m

▲ Mount Shade 507m

Glendye Lodge

Bridge of Dye

② Miller's Bog

Mill Burn

▲ Hill of Edendocher
④ 577m

▲ Hill of Duclash

Burn of Waterhead

▲ Cairn of Finglenny

⑥ Spittal Bridge

Brocky Burn

⑤
Charr

Water of Dye

Glen Dye

B974

1 km
1 mile

1. Take the path out of the car park and go on to walk a delightful track through the forest. Pass below several splendid Douglas fir, the haunt of coal tits and goldcrests. As you descend to the edge of the woodland you have your first view over moorland to Clachnaben. Once out of the trees, bear left and continue downhill beside walled beech woodland to go through a gate. Cross a footbridge over the birch-lined Mill Burn. At the Y-junction take the right fork, which takes you out into a flat moorland valley, with high land rearing up all around and Clachnaben ahead. At the next Y-junction take the right branch to cross a footbridge, which avoids a ford, and continue on. Cross two more footbridges as you head towards a large area of pine woodland.

2. Climb the stile into the trees, with a huge mound to the right, covered in pines. Follow the path as it winds round, left, of the mound. To your left, in summer, Mill Burn flows sweetly down its birch-lined bed and through lush vegetation; in winter it roars. Continue on, passing below magnificent firs, pines and birch. Then the path moves out onto the heather moorland, the path traversing

119

Coal tit

the hillside in a northerly direction. Carry on up where the way is pitched and often stepped, passing through bell heather, ling, bilberry and crowberry. Pause as the path winds left towards the tor, for a wonderful view of the lowlands, stretching away to misty hills. Climb several sections of steps up to the tor. Here walkers must decide whether to scramble, with great care, to the top of the huge protrusion of granite. If so it is best approached from the north side—the south side is slippery and precipitous. After enjoying the stunning view some walkers will want to return from the top by the same route. This walk continues on.

3. Head on from the summit on a good track towards the trig point, which stands just before a smaller tor. By-pass the latter by using the track that keeps to the left of the outcrop. Walk on along the ridge, with heather stretching away into the distance. Negotiate a wide peat hag, which might present difficulties in the winter or after heavy rain. And then go over a wide area of granite, broken down into fine grit. Look right to see several grouse butts and then climb steadily on a better path to reach the Hill of Edendocher, where you join a wide track and there are three tall gate posts.

4. Turn left and steadily descend, with care, a rough wide landrover track, where the stones can act like ball-bearings as you go. Eventually the path begins to level and it becomes slightly easier to walk. Follow the track as it keeps to the right of the Cairn of Finglenny—here you may wish to take a narrow path, on the left, which leads through heather to the top. Carry on along the main path as it winds right and climbs again. Press on along the track and follow it as it winds left and begins a steep rough descent to Charr. Here the Brocky Burn joins the Dye and there is a mountain

bothy set in a delightful hollow surrounded by the high hills, including Little Calf, Meikle Calf, Rough Bank, and Meluncart.

5. Turn left onto another wide track, remaining on the north side of the bothy. Once you have passed a small burn, turn right to descend a track towards the reservoir in Glen Dye, and then bear left with the track to walk through the glen. Continue on and as you cross the bridge below which flows the Burn of Waterhead, look upstream for a fine view of Clachnaben. Carry on along the track as it rises high above the river and then descends to curve round with it. After two miles from the bridge you pass Spitalbank plantation and roofless Spital Cottage on the other side of the Water of Dye.

6. Ignore Spital Bridge and carry on along the less well used, easy-to-walk, grassy track, with the valley becoming pleasingly wooded. Go through a gate and cross Mill Beck, in the opposite direction to that taken earlier. Retrace your outward route to the car park.

Crowberry and Bearberry

Practicals

Type of walk: This takes you through varying countryside to and from an interesting summit. Return from the summit by your outward route if the weather changes.

Distance: 10 miles/16km
Time: 5–6 hours
Maps: OS Explorers 396 & 395, OS Landranger 45

Grouse and deer shooting from August 12 to October 20—best to return by route of ascent at this time of year. For information telephone Glendye Estate 01330 850656

31

Mount Keen from Glen Mark

Park in the large car park almost at the end of the road at Invermark, grid ref 447804. To reach this take the minor road up Glen Esk from Gannochy Bridge, north of Edzell.

Mount Keen (3,077 ft/939m) is the most easterly of the Munros in Scotland. It forms an isolated dome well away from any other Munro and is only reached after a long walk in from either Glen Esk in the south or Glen Tanar to the north. The walking is, however, very straightforward on good clear tracks all the way. It is said that Queen Victoria went to the summit on horseback.

The canopy over the **Queen's Well** was built to commemorate the occasion on September 21, 1861, when members of the Queen's party including herself and Prince Albert refreshed themselves at the spring during a journey over the Mounth Road. Prince Albert died later the same year but the two events have never been connected. The water looks clear and good although full of plant life.

Queen's Well

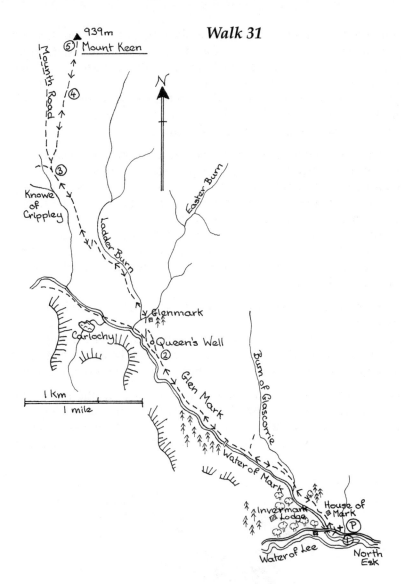

1. Go on for 200 metres along the road from the parking area to pass a small church. Take the right branch, signed 'House of Mark and Footpath to Ballater by the Mounth Road', before the bridge over the Water of Mark. Walk in front of the House of Mark, go through a gate and stroll on above the river. At this point the glen divides into Glen Mark and Glen Lee and the area is pleasantly wooded

123

with birch. Continue on through a plantation of pine and then out onto open moorland. Carry on for a mile and a quarter. At the right time of the year you should hear the calls of curlews and see oystercatchers and common sandpipers along the river. In spring you might spot ring ouzels feeding on the stony, heathery mounds in the valley bottom. Look also for patches of yellow petty whin flowering among the expanses of heather.

2. Continue on and then, when you can see a curious domed structure, the Queen's Well, follow a grassy path to it. Then go on along the continuing grassy path to rejoin the main track once more and carry on to pass, to the left of the last house in the glen. Ford the Easter Burn on irregular stepping stones and, soon afterwards, the Ladder Burn on a tubular metal grid. Carry on the track as it turns and, with the burn to your right, follow it as it begins to climb, slanting up the steep slope and finally zigzagging up onto the plateau by the Knowe of Crippley.

3. Press on up the obvious track to a fork, where you turn right. Ignore two cairns which mark short alternative paths on the right, and follow the main track ahead, through an eroded and winding cat's cradle of minor paths. Go on where the track bears slightly right and ignore the more indistinct branch which goes straight ahead.

4. Ascend the now obvious motorway-like track up the mountain. Look for pebbles of agate and jasper lying in the track. Soon you cross the final plateau where you will find an old boundary marker stone, set upright and with the letter B carved on its northern face.

Pretty Whin

Go on past the stone and climb the final rocky mound to reach the trig point on the top. Here you will want to pause to enjoy the distant views of the Cairngorms and Lochnagar.

5. Then retrace your steps down over the wide heather moorland to the valley of the Ladder Burn and back down into Glen Mark. The cliffs opposite look spectacular from this viewpoint, with the small lochan, Carlochy of Mark, nestling beneath them. Soon the Queen's Well is reached. Beyond continue on the level way down Glen Mark. Ahead is a large pyramidal monument on the Hill of Rowan. Descend, gently, through the wooded part of the glen and back to the car park.

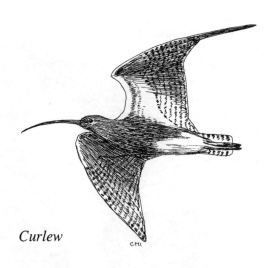

Curlew

Practicals

Type of walk: This is an easy but long walk to a Munro, taking you through birch and pine woodland and then over open moorland, on generally good tracks.

Distance: 11 ½ miles/17.5km
Time: 5–6 hours
Maps: OS Explorer 395, OS Landranger 44

32

Falls of Unich and of Damff

Park in the large car park at the end of the public road at Invermark, grid ref 447804. This is reached by the minor road up Glen Esk, which leaves the B966 at Gannochy Bridge, 1 ¼ miles/2km north of Edzell.

The Water of Unich and its tributaries drain a high moorland basin between Glenesk and Glen Clova. A considerable volume of water pours down the narrow valley between Hunt Hill and Craig Maskeldie, giving rise to the **two spectacular waterfalls** and a gorge containing a whole series of small falls and waterslides.

Invermark Castle dates from 1526 and was built to guard the vital pass from Glen Esk to Deeside (the Mounth Road). It was altered in 1605. Today it is a dramatic ruin.

Falls of Unich

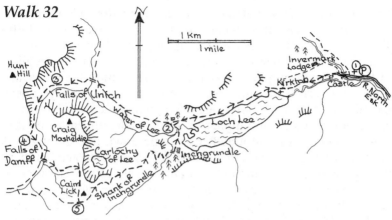

1. From the car park walk on along the road past the church and turn left at the fork to cross the bridge over the Water of Mark. At the next fork, again take the left branch. Invermark Castle is on the left a short distance further on. As the ruins are dangerous—just view. Continue along the track beside the Water of Lee, through birch woodland with, in summer, an abundant ground flora which includes melancholy thistle. Go through the kissing gate beside the cattle grid and walk downhill to come out of the trees near a cluster of buildings called Kirkton. Ahead, and to the left, are the ruins of the church founded on this site, in the early 7th century, by St Drostan. The remains you can see were built in the late 16th and early 17th century. Beyond the wall of the church lies Loch Lee. Follow the track along its north shore, where in summer you are likely to spot sand and house martins, swallows and pied wagtails. Listen here for the raucous screaming of peregrines as they circle above the cliffs to the right.

2. At the end of the loch ignore the track on the left, which goes down to Inchgrundle, and continue up the valley past a small plantation and an empty cottage called Glenlee. Pass a small shed with a corrugated iron roof. The track climbs and bends to the right, above the Water of Lee. Across the valley you can see the splendid Falls of Unich where the Water of Unich descends from its narrow valley between Hunt Hill and Craig Maskeldie. At the Y-junction take the left path and cross the Water of Lee on a solid new footbridge. The path beyond winds along the hillside and then comes down to traverse the grassy flood plain between the two rivers, Unich and Lee.

127

3. Near the waterfall it begins to re-ascend the valleyside to reach a small grassy stance from where you have a fine view of the falls. Then climb steeply up, pausing to admire the hollow cut out of the rock above the main fall—where the water boils in great turmoil—to find a contouring path above the gorge behind the waterfall. There is a variety of paths to choose from—some take you near the edge and provide views of the gorge and the turbulent river, while others, wider and higher up the hillside, appear to be less white-knuckle. All join together to come down into a delightful hidden valley, grassy at first and then full of moraine and boulders through which winds the path on an intricate route. The rock is mica schist and in places the ground shines silver with fragments. Above the moraine the path—maybe an old stalkers' path—slants up the valleyside on a wide shelf below birch woodland and then it turns aside into a small side valley near the top. Cross a boggy area and climb up the small dry valley until you emerge onto heather and peat.

4. Cross the moor for a short distance and then take a side path, left, to look at the Falls of Damff. These are much less accessible than the Falls of Unich; you can scramble down a steep path to admire the short upper fall and you can see the lower fall from above. Return to the main path and continue over the moor until you spot a substantial bridge below to your left. Go down to it and cross. Follow the indistinct path, going uphill through another boggy area, and then it reaches drier ground on the bank of the burn and improves. Follow it upwards towards the skyline. Where it divides take the left branch which heads for higher ground. Cross a few wet areas, with care, to come to the lip of a corrie. If you look down you can see the lochan Carlochy of Lee below, cradled in the corrie, and then out beyond the corrie is Loch Lee and misty hills stretching away to Mount Battock. Continue

Short-eared owl

along the path as it turns right and crosses drier rocky ground, above the corrie, to the summit of Cairn Lick, with hardly any climbing involved.

5. Look for the estate track, 330 ft/100m beyond the summit, where you turn left. Follow the zigzags down the Shank of Inchgrundle eventually coming into open larch woodland above the farm of Inchgrundle. Cross the Inchgrundle burn on another new wooden bridge and turn left to go past the farm buildings to join a wide track across the valley. At the far side turn right on the track along the side of Loch Lee, retracing your outward path to Invermark.

Bog asphodel and sphagnum

Practicals

Type of walk: There is a clear path for much of the way, although take care with route finding up on the rather featureless moors at the top. It is very steep near the waterfalls and care must be taken especially with children The remainder of the walk is on estate tracks. Dogs must be kept on leads and you are asked to avoid the area beyond Inchgrundle during the main shooting season between August 12 and October 20. For more information contact the Invermark Estate on 01356 670208. It is a member of the East Grampian Deer Management Group.

Distance: 10 miles/16.5km
Time: 4–5 hours
Maps: OS Explorer 395, OS Landranger 44

33

Tarfside and Hill of Rowan

Park in the large car park (with toilets) on the left as you drive up the glen at Tarfside, grid ref 494796. To reach this take the minor road up Glen Esk, which leaves the B966 at Gannochy Bridge, 2km north of Edzell.

On the top of the **Hill of Rowan** stands the Maule Monument, a conical stone tower with a small pillar on the top. It has an entrance sealed with an iron gate. It was erected, in 1866, by the first Baron Panmure in memory of seven members of the Maule family and also of Lady Ramsay McDonald, the Lady Christian Maule and Lord Panmure himself.

Bridge over N. Esk near Dalbrack

Drostan's Cross Stone stands beside the path over the moorland. It is a simple Latin cross incised on its north face in a style typical of the Columbian Church. It was probably connected to St Drostan's religious establishment and is said to have been moved, in the early 19th century, to its present site from elsewhere in the glen. Local legend has it that Robert the Bruce planted his Royal Standard on it before a battle to subdue the powerful Red Comyn, Earl of Buchan, in the winter of 1306.

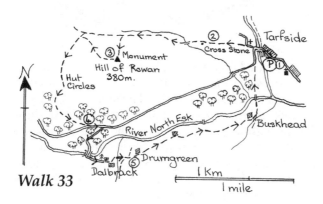

Walk 33

1. Turn left out of the car park and continue past a row of cottages to cross the old stone bridge over the Water of Tarf. Turn right, immediately, along a road signed 'Milton', with the Episcopal Church of St Drostan on your right. Where the road turns sharp right go straight on along a grassy fenced outrake. Pass through a gate at the end and follow the delightful grassy track out onto the moor.

2. Look for two very prominent ancient cairns on the left of the path and approximately 150m beyond the second one, look for the small cross stone beside the path. Cross the Burn of Rowan. Carry on along the narrowing valley and as you approach the col at the top, take a clear track on the left continuing uphill through heather to the monument. The view from the top is splendid, encompassing Glens Lee and Mark at the head of Glen Esk, with Mount Keen beyond Glen Mark and Mount Battock to the east.

3. Turn right to walk west, away from the monument, soon to descend through heather and then grassy areas with ruined dykes (walls) around the edges. Keep a lookout for raptors—you might spot hen

Hen harrier

harrier, short-eared owl, kestrel, buzzard and golden eagle. When you reach a low wall and a wooden post, turn left down a clear grassy track between ruined walls. The stone heaps you pass may be hut circles and the remains of an old field system shown on the map. Go through a gate and follow the clearest track along by grouse butts. At a Y-junction just before the last butt, turn right along an indistinct path shortly to join a clearer path lower down. Turn left and wind round the grassy hillside into birch woodland and finally out to the road at a gate.

4. Turn left and walk for 300m to a junction. Take the right branch, signposted 'Dalbrack and Drumgreen' and also 'Public footpath to Lethnot and Brechin', passing through birch woodland. Cross the River North Esk, which here is full of rapids and potholes, on a delightful stone bridge—there is a bench by the river where you might like to eat your lunch. Carry on along the metalled road until it ends in a farmyard. Take the track to the left going downhill through the yard—the right one passes in front of the farmhouse. Cross the Burn of Dalbrack and follow the track round to a fork where the right of way goes right—you however take the left branch. There is an East Grampian Deer Management Group sign here, asking you to stick to rights of way between August 12 and October 20.

5. At the next junction take the right fork along a grassy track, which passes the ruins of Drumgreen and runs along between the valley grazing and the open hill. There are good views of the Hill of Rowan, and its monument, across the valley. At more ruins the track divides; take the obvious branch which goes to the right through a metal gate and skirts the edge of the moor, with a wall

on the left. Carry on through another gate, past lots of old settlements. Press on along the track as it climbs gently. It is grassy and gives pleasing walking and wonderful open views up and down the valley from the brow. Go through another metal gate and pass Buskhead farm. Beyond another gate, turn left down the hill to a wooden footbridge over the North Esk. Follow the track ahead through birch woodland and out onto the road. Turn right and return over the Water of Tarf bridge to the car park.

Kestrel

Practicals

Type of walk: A very pleasant mainly low level walk on good tracks, giving fine open views. Probably best avoided between August 12 and October 20 when shooting is in progress, except on Sundays. All dogs on the lead or at heel.

Distance: 5 ½ miles/9km
Time: 3 hours
Maps: OS Explorer 395, OS Landranger 44

34

River North Esk from Edzell

If you wish to make this a circular, or a 'there and back' walk, use on-street parking close to the post office at Edzell, grid ref, 601689. There is also a car park north of the village, grid ref 599694. If you prefer to make this a linear walk and use two cars the second should be parked grid ref, 588739, which is a lay-by on the minor road running north up Glen Esk from Gannochy Bridge.

This **lovely riverside walk** starts at the pleasing village of Edzell. At first sight the North Esk is wide and shallow and the surrounding land gently undulating and wooded. Then, very soon, the path climbs steadily above a magnificent gorge through which the river surges and foams. Just before Gannochy Bridge the fenced path enables you to look down into an immense ravine which confines the tempestuous burn. Beyond the bridge the path continues beside the river through delightful

Rocks of Solitude, R. North Esk

mixed woodland, with more spectacular views. Then when you reach a level area, where the river flows lazily past meadows and you think all its impetuosity is tamed, it still holds its main glory ahead. Here the path takes you through a stunning high sheer-sided gorge, where the North Esk crashes down waterfalls, cascades over hard rocky protuberances and swirls and dances on its way through a tree-lined wonderland. The reason for all this wonderful scenery is that the walk crosses the Highland line boundary fault where the rocks are all hard and mixed up.

Walk 34

1. Leave Edzell's main street by a narrow lane beside the post office where a sign on its wall directs you to the riverside and the Shakkin' Brig'. Pass a car repair works and go through a picnic area and turn left soon to pass, but not cross, the elegant footbridge firmly held in place by two long steel hawsers attached to the riverbank. The railed way soon rises above the river and then continues through a narrow strip of fine beech trees, from where you can see the coloured boulders that form the bed of the waterway. As the path nears Gannochy Bridge the river crashes through a very deep red sandstone gorge.

2. At the road turn right and, facing the oncoming traffic, go over the bridge with care. Beyond, cross the road and pass through a wooden gate in the wall. A narrow path leads on, high above the river, with fine woodland to your right where you might spot a red squirrel. Keep to the riverside path as it passes a stately house, named The Burn, now a study centre. Wind round a deepish gully and then return to the riverside to continue. On the opposite bank rich pasture land stretches away. Then the path, still deep in woodland, climbs

135

high above the river once more and leads you on into a dramatic gorge, where the North Esk rages furiously against its confining sides. Here you will want to pause and use your camera.

3. The main path then heads away from the watercourse and joins a road close to the lay-by where you might have left a second car. Here a decision has to be made, whether to retrace your steps to Gannochy Bridge or to turn right to walk for 1 ½ miles along the road where you will encounter some traffic. At the road end, turn right along the Edzell road to cross the bridge and retrace your outward route to the village.

Practicals

Type of walk: Good footpaths along the whole length of the river, with some high above deep gorges. The road return to the bridge is beside or through woodland. From Gannochy Bridge there is a way of return along the east bank of the river where you take a narrow path by a telegraph pole just before the bridge, which climbs uphill to join a wider track. At first the path through the beeches is a delight. After a mile it narrows and continues with fields to the left and a steep bank to the right. Two fields further on it descends an unmarked muddy steepish bank to the riverside. It then continues along a rough path and across a pebbly section of the riverbed (which might be under water if the river is high). It then goes pleasingly on through a wooded area covered with wood anemones in the spring, to the side of the Shakkin' Brig', which you cross to return to Edzell. If this route is for you, you may wish to start off this way so that you can check before you have gone too far whether the way is passable. If not use the west bank for both your outward and return route.

Distance: 6 ½ miles/10.5km
Time: 3 hours
Maps: OS Explorer 389, OS Landrangers 44 and 45

35

The White & Brown Caterthuns

Park in the small car park, grid ref 553662, on the highest part of the road between the two forts, 4 ½ miles north-west of Brechin or 3 ½ miles south-west of Edzell.

The twin hill forts, the White Caterthun and the Brown Caterthun, perch on the top of two low rounded hills on the north side of the Strathmore valley. Both are strategically placed and it would have been difficult for the occupants to be surprised by an enemy. They are believed to have been hilltop towns.

From the twin forts look down on the **rich farmland** of the broad valley below—an area of quiet beauty with tree-lined fields and well kept towns and villages. Through the valley meander the rivers, slow-moving now after their rush, in cascades and waterfalls, from the surrounding hills.

White Caterthun

Walk 35

1. From the car park and picnic area set off up the clear, well kept grassy path that ascends through heather to the White Caterthun (979 ft/ 298m). Away to the left the slopes support scattered pine, spruce and larch. As you go enjoy the steadily improving views. Continue up the easy-to-walk path to enter the extensive oval hollow, surrounded by a derelict dyke (wall). Follow any of the little paths through the centre and then walk around the perimeter, pausing often to take in the superb view over to the hills about the Angus glens. Peer over the dyke to see the small ramparts. Find a corner to sit in the sun and enjoy the atmosphere of this high level ancient site. The White Caterthun was probably built by the Picts in the 1st century AD, or maybe earlier. Then return down the slope.

2. Cross the road and take the path, a rougher and longer way, leading beside a fence towards the Brown Caterthun. The way climbs steadily over heather moorland to the top (967 ft/287m) from where you can see south-east across the lovely valley of Strathmore and, west, across to the Angus hills. Again you will want to linger, especially when the air is perfumed by the heather. The Brown Caterthun is slightly lower and more extensive than its neighbour and is easily recognised by its dark brown heather and its six concentric earth banks. These multiple banks gave added strength to the naturally defensive position of the site. However, there are, unusually, a large number of gaps in the banks for a defensive site. If all the gaps were part of the original works the site might have had a more complex function. Similar sites in other parts of the country had ceremonial functions and were built about five thousand years ago. The Brown Caterthun was abandoned before the White Caterthun was developed. Return to the car park by your outward route.

Common heather or ling

Practicals

Type of walk: A visit to both forts is a delight. Short and moderately easy.

Distance: 2 miles/3km
Time: 1–2 hours
Maps: OS Explorer 389, OS Landranger 44

36

Airlie Monument from Cortachy

Park in Cortachy car park, grid ref 392598. To reach this turn right off Clova Road, B955, just before Dykehead, in the direction of Brechin and Edzell. The un-signposted car park lies on the left just before the primary school.

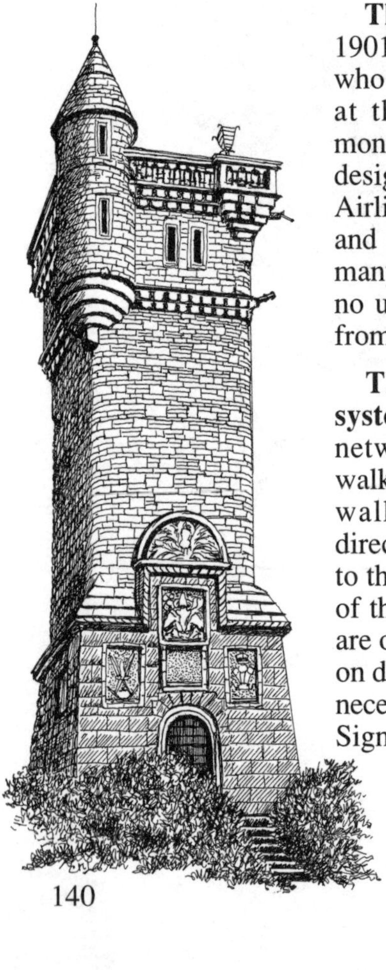

The Airlie monument was erected in 1901 in memory of the 11th Earl of Airlie who was killed in action in the Boer War at the Battle of Diamond Hill. The monument stands 654 ft/21m high and the design is of the character of the tower at Airlie Castle. It is an impressive landmark and so prominent that it can be seen for many miles around. The monument has no use but the walk to it and the views from its foot are most rewarding.

The Cortachy and Dykehead path system has been designed to provide a network of attractive, easily followed walks through a variety of terrain. All the walks are waymarked, with yellow directional arrows. You are asked to keep to these routes and to respect the privacy of the residents on the estate. The walks are open all year, with the exception that, on days when there is shooting, it may be necessary to close part or all of the network Signs will be displayed at such times.

Airlie Monument

140

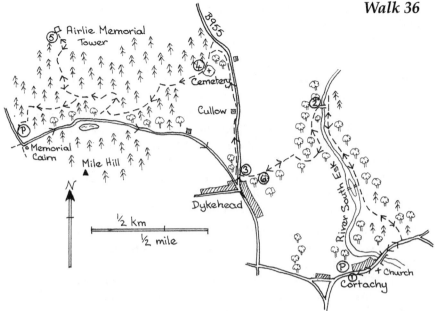

1. From the car park, cross the road and turn left to walk the pavement. Go past several formidable gates. One gives access to Cortachy, The Glens and Old Kirriemuir church, set just within the grounds of Cortachy Castle. Cross the bridge over the River South Esk and, 80m beyond, go through ornamental gates on the left (north) side of the road. Once through, continue on the waymarked pleasing, grassy path to pass below lofty pines and firs, and great banks of rhododendrons. The path then comes close to the river and you can look down on the Esk, tumbling through its valley. Ignore two wooden footbridges, which are private. They span the river, first crossing to an island and then to the opposite bank. Follow the path as it climbs up above a fishing stance and comes to another footbridge which you do cross.

2. Carry on along the path, beyond, as it winds left, climbing through more magnificent woodland. At a waymark the path bears right, away from the river, and then goes on along the edge of the trees. Where the woodland ends, go through a gate on the left to walk a delightful grassy way, enclosed between two fences, with woodland still to your left, and open pasture to the right. From here you can see the Airlie monument on its hill surrounded by conifers. Pass a

141

seat strategically positioned to enjoy a good view over the forest and its clearings. Go on through more trees to come to a narrow road (B955) just outside Dykehead.

3. Cross the road and into more woodland. Walk right, keeping parallel with the road. Emerge from the trees and go-on on the waymarked way, with a fenced pasture to your left and, to your right, the B-road, edged with sycamores. Where you reach Cullen cottage, join the road and once past rejoin the path along the banking and press on to its end. Follow the waymark, directing you left, to enter beech woodland and walk, at first parallel with the road, and then moving deeper into the trees. The path climbs gradually and curves left through the trees to meet the access road to Cortachy Cemetery. Turn left and walk to the gates of the burial ground.

4. Just before the gates, turn right to walk through more trees, with a field to your left. Here you might spot a pair of bullfinches. Follow the track uphill, then where it winds left through Scots pine and larch. At the T-junction, turn right and go on through pines. Ignore the waymarked left turn and stroll on. As you go look down the fire breaks to your left to see delightful views of Glen Prosen far below. Carry on along the steadily climbing track to emerge onto a glorious open sward, with the Airlie monument ahead standing proud. The view beyond over Glen Clova and Glen Prosen, with higher hills in the distance, is stunning. To the south lies a wonderful patchwork of fields and woodland. From the monument you can walk on along the ridge for as far as you wish.

5. To continue, return from the monument by retracing your outward route and take the turn, now on your right, ignored on your upward climb. Press on down this pleasing grassy track as it descends through more pine woodland to join the narrow road to Glen Prosen. Turn left and

Bullfinches

142

walk on to pass the small cairn-like monument to Captain Robert Falcon Scott and Edward Wilson who died in the Antarctic, trying to reach the south pole. The legend on the cairn says that both men liked to walk in and around Glen Prosen. Walk on into the village of Dykehead to turn left onto the Glen Clova road. In a few steps take the unsigned path, on the right, through woodland—this is the path you walked earlier.

6. Very soon you reach a Y-junction where you should remember to take the waymarked left branch to stroll the delightful fenced grassy path. Continue on, retracing your outward route to return to the parking area.

Primroses and violets

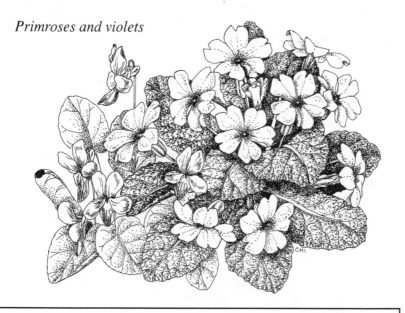

Practicals

Type of walk: A fine walk with gentle climbs on good paths, through a wonderful variety of woodland, pasture, riverside and high moorland.

Distance: 7 miles/11.35km
Time: 3 ½ hours
Maps: OS Explorer 381, OS Landranger 44/54

37

Glen Prosen to Glen Clova:

The Minister's Path

Park by Glen Prosen church, grid ref 327657. To reach this take the B955, signed 'The Glens', from Kirriemuir to Dykehead. Here take, to the left, the minor road, signed 'Glen Prosen', for 5 miles/ 8km.

The name **Minister's Path** comes from the time when the minister of the parish did walk from one church to another to conduct services. As you do the walk ponder on how he managed in the winter.

This walk can be done with two cars, one left by Glen Prosen church and the other in limited parking in Glen Clova, grid ref 357697. Or you may wish to retrace your steps, making it a there and back walk. Four kilometres, left,

Glen Prosen
Church

through Glen Clova, lies Clova village where there is a church, an inn and a cafe. The Minister's Path is a clear, easy route. It is a right of way,

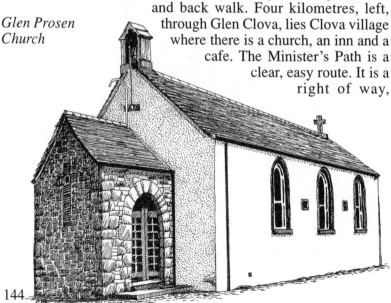

with a Scottish Rights of Way Society (SRWS) sign, both at the start and at the end. It can be walked at any time of year, weather permitting, because it is a right-of-way. Grouse shooting does take place from August 12 through into autumn so do give this due consideration. There is no shooting on Sundays.

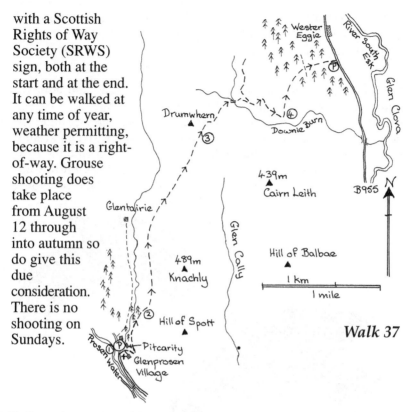

Walk 37

1. Follow the track, with a SRWS sign, which passes between the church at Glen Prosen and the Burn of Inchmill. Ignore the side turns, right and left, which lead to houses, and go ahead with the track as it bends right and crosses in front of a cottage named Pitcarity. Beyond a gate, walk out onto the hill. The path winds round in a hairpin, climbing quite steeply, and then runs along the upper edge of a conifer plantation, where in summer, the slopes to the right are covered with heather, sprinkled with harebells and tormentil. Look here for siskins and coal tits.

2. Go through the next gate onto the open fell and climb gently along the valley side. Beyond an isolated farm, on the far side of the burn, the valley opens out into a wide moorland basin, ringed to the north-west with distant peaks. Pass through a row of grouse butts and continue to the top of the ridge.

3. Cross a fence at a gate to begin your long descent on a rougher

track into Glen Clova. Take the bridge over the Downie burn and ascend briefly on the far side. Carry on down to pass through more grouse butts and as you go enjoy the fine view of the impressive corries that have been gouged out of the far side of Glen Clova.

4. Press on down the path as it makes a wide zigzag and enters a plantation at a gate. Walk on down the grassy track as it curves round inside the woodland. Cross a track and carry straight on down to a locked deer gate. Take a small path left to a high kissing gate, with a SRWS sign through the fence, and step onto the road to join your second vehicle. Or you may wish to turn left to walk the quiet road for 2 ½ miles/4km to reach the village of Clova. Otherwise retrace your steps to Glen Prosen.

Red grouse

Practicals

Type of walk: A pleasing airy walk in summer. It could be quite different in winter when there might be rain, gales and snow. Be prepared.

Distance: 3 ½ miles/5.8km one way
Time: 2–3 hours one way
Maps: OS Explorer 388, OS Landranger 44

NB *It should not be necessary to make enquiries about times and days of shooting but if you wish to, telephone Airlie Estates 01575 550230 or Glenprosen Estate 01575 540314*

38

Loch Brandy, Glen Clova

Park in the large car park by the Clova Inn, grid ref 326731. To reach this leave Kirriemuir by the B955, signed 'The Glens', then follow the signs for Glen Clova.

Corries. Snow and ice accumulates in a mountain basin. Eventually, increasing pressure of more snow and ice causes part of the mass to move downhill and flow slowly to lower levels. As more ice moves down to the basin it tends to rotate, and wears a deep hollow, with the help of abrasion by rocks frozen into the base of the ice. Some of the ice freezes on to the back wall of the basin and, as it moves forward, plucks rock away, causing the wall to be worn back and leaving a steep face. Also water in tiny cracks in the rock freezes and expands loosening the rock this too making it easier to pluck. This final result is an 'armchair' feature known as a corrie.

Loch Brandy

1. From the car park, go uphill behind the inn, keeping to the right of the bunkhouse and then to the left of the old school, where there is a Scottish Rights of Way Society (SRWS) sign to Glen Esk. Climb quite steeply through open birch woodland to cross a burn on a stout metal plank bridge. Go over a stile in the fence onto the open hill, following a path that climbs steeply towards the skyline and is boggy in places. Ignore an obvious right turn which crosses the burn. Carry on, with the burn to your right, soon to climb beside a line of ancient fence posts.

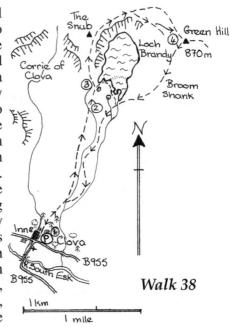

Walk 38

Eventually the gradient eases and the path, now copiously cairned, goes straight ahead over a broad, gently sloping area of heather moor.

2. Ahead are two spectacular cliff-girt corries, the wide Corrie of Clova on the left and the narrower Corrie of Loch Brandy on the right. Carry on along the path as it appears to head for a narrow spur between them, which is called The Snub. Follow the path as it runs up towards the edge of the spur and then go on along the slopes of moraine to the right of The Snub. Suddenly Loch Brandy is below you, cradled in its deep hollow beneath steep cliff walls. Follow the path which winds down through hummocks of moraine and scattered pools to the loch shore. Pause here to enjoy the pleasing view, where you might also see common gulls—probably attracted by sandwich remains!

3. Go back up from the loch shore to the top of the moraine slope below The Snub and take the path round right to climb up to its summit (2421 ft/837m). The path is very steep and rough but it enables you to gain height quickly to reach the cairn on the top. The view is superb: Dreish and Mayar are behind to the left, and

148

full left is Lochnagar. Directly ahead is the broad cone of Mount Keen. Follow the good path over short grass and bilberry. The cliffs of the corrie are badly eroded here, whole sections having fallen away, so stay well back from the edge. Go on where you might see a kestrel playing on the breeze. Then descend gently to cross a boggy burn. On the far side, where the main path veers left, take the distinct small path on the right. This narrower way follows the corrie edge at a safe distance and gives good views. Where it comes right to the edge and begins to descend, move away left away from the edge and cross the delightful short turf to rejoin the main track as it ascends to the summit of Green Hill, (2630 ft/870m).

4. Turn right (south) at the cairn on the summit and follow the pleasant track round the other side of the corrie and down over the spur, Broom Shank, which is a much gentler slope than The Snub. Once down at corrie level cross the outflow on stones and join the path that has come round the shore of the loch. Continue downhill until you cross the burn just above the trees and rejoin your outward path.

Kestrel

Practicals

Type of walk: A strenuous but very enjoyable walk with excellent views and good paths all the way. The path to the top of Green Hill could be missed in low cloud so do not venture up here without a compass. If the weather deteriorates you may wish to take the winding path along the loch shore and, in less than ¼ mile/½km, join a wide path leading downwards. Grouse shooting on the Airlie Estate (01575 550230) is from August 12 to the end of October. Ask at the Clova Hotel if unsure—they can give information on where it is best to walk.

Distance: 5 ½ miles/9km
Time: 3–4 hours
Maps: OS Explorer 388, OS Landranger 44

39

Mayar and Driesh

Park at the forestry car park at Braedownie, Glen Doll, grid ref 284762. To reach this leave Kirriemuir by the B955, signed to 'The Glens'. At the Clova Inn turn left and drive for about 4 miles on up the valley to the road end. There are two roads through the valley, both B955. Most people drive up the left side, which has the wider road.

Mayar (3,043 ft/928m) and **Driesh** (3,105 ft/947m) are an inseparable pair of Munros, standing back from the steep edges of Glen Doll at the head of Glen Clova. Mayar is a rise on the southern edge of the Mounth Plateau and is a splendid place from which to view the geography of the area. To the north is high bleak moorland culminating in Lochnagar. To the south are more rounded hills separated by deep ice-carved glens. The effect of the ice, gouging out corries with their flat floors and enclosing cliffs, is much more obvious from Driesh.

Glen Doll and Corrie Fee are enclosed by a continuous if broken, line of cliffs. The rock is mica schist and rich in alpine plants. It is part of the

*Driesh, from
Glen Doll*

Caenlochan national nature reserve. Without searching in some alarmingly exposed places walkers are unlikely to find any of the especial rarities such as yellow oxytropis or the alpine milk vetch, but purple saxifrage is common beside the path of ascent and at the right time of year all the other usual mountain flowers are abundant.

Walk 39

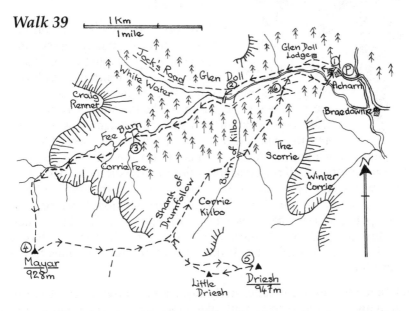

1. Leave the car park at the west end, opposite to the entrance, and walk up the track to a complex five-way junction. Here, bear slightly left and downhill just outside the wall of Acharn farm and to the left of a sign saying 'Forest Walks'. One field on along this way, ignore the junction on the left, and go on up the track, following white waymarker posts. Stride the track from where there are splendid open views of the burn, White Water, down to your left, and across to the magnificent cirque of cliffs enclosing Glen Doll and Corrie Fee. In spring the banks are carpeted with primroses, violets and wood sorrel; curlews and oyster catchers call from the fields in the valley and in the evenings you may see woodcock roding.

2. On reaching a turning circle, ignore the signposted 'Jock's Road. Braemar 14 miles', an ancient Mounth road, and go straight on along the forest track and then down to a bridge over the White

151

Purple Saxifrage

Water. Beyond, carry on beside the Fee Burn through an area of clear fell and then back into the forest. The track then becomes a well made path, which eventually leaves the forest at a stile and gate at the mouth of Corrie Fee.

3. Pass the sign saying that you are now entering the nature reserve and go down the path into the corrie and across a line of moraines, with flat boggy grassland on either side. At the back of the corrie the path begins to climb the headwall, where the Fee Burn comes down in a series of splendid waterfalls, and the path zigzags up on the left of these. Cross a tributary burn and wind left, then contour round to cross another burn. Climb a small rockstep and follow a wide shelf round towards the waterfalls. Here purple saxifrage grows on the rocks. Climb easily out at the top of the headwall into a shallow basin beyond and pause to look back down into Corrie Fee and Glen Doll. Then follow the path by the burn and up through a hummocky basin, until it crosses a tributary. It then turns left, and continues to the summit of Mayar.

4. Leave the summit in an easterly direction, following the decrepit remains of a fence and a path like a motorway. About half a mile further on the path joins a more robust fence and a signpost, pointing right for 'Glenprosen and Glenisla by Kilbo Path'. Ignore this and carry on ahead, walking beside the fence to its end. Here there is a path going off left and marked by a large cairn. This is your return path, it should be remembered but ignored for the present. Now go on down to the col, with Corrie Kilbo to your left, and then climb up onto Driesh at the far side, remaining on the broad path. As the angle eases, follow the path which by-passes the top of Little Driesh and brings

Dotterel

152

you out onto the col before the final gentle ascent to the main summit. In spring and summer look for dotterel here. The trig point on top of Driesh is surrounded by a small sheltering wall.

5. Return by your route of ascent, perhaps going over the top of Little Driesh this time, and then down the col to the cairn noted earlier. Then follow the long gentle path down the side of Corrie Kilbo. It traverses the side of a ridge called Shank of Drumfollow above the deep glaciated corrie. Eventually the path comes down to the trees and then soon goes into the forest at a gate in the deer fence. Wind down to cross the Kilbo Burn and various minor burns. At a forest track, cross and take the continuing path going on down.

6. Turn left at the next forest track and go on round a hairpin bend in the track to take the small path off left, continuing your original line downhill. Turn right on the path at the bottom by the river and follow this path until it joins another forest track at a gate. Go through and turn left, cross the bridge over the White Water and turn right onto the track you walked out on. Follow it up past Acharn farm and back down to the car park.

Ring ouzel

Practicals

Type of walk: Generally easy walking on mainly good tracks and over short vegetation. It is steep up the corrie headwall but nowhere difficult. Both mountains are Munros and proper footwear, waterproofs etc are essential. Even easy Munros should be treated with respect.

Distance: 9 miles/14.5km
Time: 5–6 hours
Maps: OS Explorer 388, OS Landranger 44

NB *For enquiries about the walk, telephone 01575 550230*

Glen Isla

Park on a grassy verge before the bridge to Linns, grid ref 193698. To reach this leave the B951 by a turn, going north-east, at Meikle Forter to pass fine Forter Castle. Continue in the same direction along the narrow road through Glen Isla, with the Isla river beside you to the right. Drive to the end of the tarmacked way and bear right along a rough track for a quarter of a mile to the grassy verge, edging the river.

Alpine Lady's Mantle is found only in mountainous parts at altitudes not lower than 400 ft/122m. The leaves are cut to the base into five or seven oblong leaflets, the underside is clothed with white silky hairs. The tiny flowers are yellow and appear to nestle among the leaves.

Canness Glen from head of Glen Isla

The pretty **mountain pansy** grows in profusion along the side of the track into the depths of Glen Isla. Its flowers, larger than those of the wild pansy, rise up on slender stems from underground runners. They occur in various colour forms—deep purple with yellow eye, or all yellow, or something between. It occurs in grass on mountain sides in lime-rich areas.

Caenlochan national nature reserve (CNNR) is one of the best areas for arctic-alpine plants in Britain. The rock is lime-rich mica schist and is exposed in the fine cliffs enclosing the Caenlochan and Canness Glens. The best places for the plants are on inaccessible ledges out of reach of the deer.

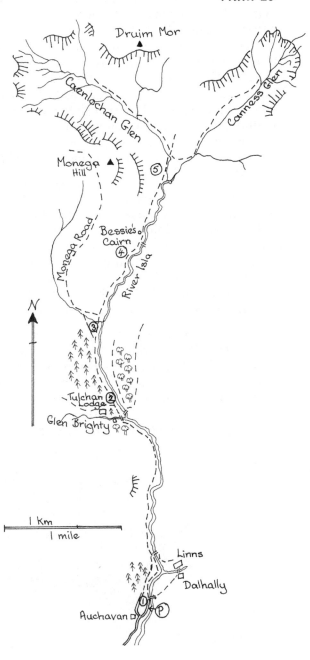

1. Do not cross the bridge but continue on the way, the Monega Path, marked by a Scottish Rights of Way Society footpath sign. This grassy track hugs the riverbank as it makes a delightful wide curve and here you should see dippers. At the next bridge, which you also ignore, the delectable way joins the reinforced track, through the glen. Continue ahead with high rounded hills in front of you. Soon you can see Tulchan Lodge tucked into its mixed woodland, with a large conifer plantation stretching beyond. Cross the next footbridge over the burn coming down from Glen Brighty. Ignore the gates on your left, which give access to Tulchan Lodge, and go on along the Monega path, remaining throughout this walk on the left side of the Isla Burn.

2. Leave the mixed planting around the Lodge and go on past the plantation, the mature trees appearing rather small against the high hills. Look for Alpine lady's mantle growing along the track, reminding you just how high up you are, even though you are in the glen. And then as the way curves gently you can see, in stark contrast to the rounded hills, the pointed crags and steep sides of Druim Mor, which enclose the austere glens of Caenlochan and Canness. If the sun is shining on cliffs the view is awesome.

3. Then you reach the signpost which points out the route taken by the Monega Path. It climbs the steep slopes onto Monega Hill, Little Glas Maol and onwards. This is the point, during the shooting season (August 12–October 20) when you are asked not to proceed further into the glen, but you can of course climb the Monega Path. This walk, outside the shooting season, continues along the picturesque way, with sheer, craggy slopes ahead and the dancing

Alpine Ladies' Mantle

156

River Isla beside you on your right. Look for deer up on the grassy sides of the valley as you go.

4. Carry on the easy-to-follow track, where in late spring and summer the sward is spangled with mountain pansies, until you come to just below a stone four-sided seat, Bessie's Cairn, dated 1852. Choose the side out of the wind for your picnic. Sit here and enjoy the view, all part of the CNNR. The path continues almost to the foot of the glen to a footbridge over the confluence of the Caenlochan and Canness burns. From here you may wish to follow a path into either glen.

5. Then return by your outward route.

Mountain Pansies

Practicals

Type of walk: A glorious easy walk, with no chance of getting lost. Take extra warm clothing as the temperature steadily drops as you walk towards the two glens at the head of Glen Isla

Distance:	5 miles/8km return, to where the Monega path leaves Glen Isla and 6 ½ miles/10.5km return to Bessie's seat.
Time:	3 hours
Maps:	OS Explorer 388, OS Landranger 43 and 44

NB Although the head of the glen is a NNR there is deer stalking—either just use the Monega path or ring the head stalker for information on 01575 582321.

Walking Scotland Series
from
Clan Books

MARY WELSH has already compiled walkers' guides to each of the areas listed; material for guides covering the remaining parts of Scotland is being gathered for publication in future volumes.

Titles published so far:

1. WALKING THE ISLE OF ARRAN
2. WALKING THE ISLE OF SKYE
3. WALKING WESTER ROSS
4. WALKS IN PERTHSHIRE
5. WALKING THE WESTERN ISLES
6. WALKING ORKNEY
7. WALKING SHETLAND
8. WALKING THE ISLES OF ISLAY, JURA AND COLONSAY
9. WALKING GLENFINNAN: THE ROAD TO THE ISLES
10. WALKING THE ISLES OF MULL, IONA, COLL AND TIREE
11. WALKING DUMFRIES AND GALLOWAY
12. WALKING ARGYLL AND BUTE
13. WALKING DEESIDE, DONSIDE AND ANGUS
14. WALKING THE TROSSACHS, LOCH LOMONDSIDE AND THE CAMPSIE FELLS
15. WALKING GLENCOE, LOCHABER AND THE GREAT GLEN

Books in this series can be ordered through booksellers anywhere. In the event of difficulty write to
Clan Books, The Cross, DOUNE, FK16 6BE, Scotland.